LOVES ME,
IN LIFE'S GAME
YOU CAN BE THE

THE PORTABLE P   SOLVER

Discover . . .

- Which relationship is responsible for most of your difficulties in life
- What three major relationship problems surface before you are two years old
- Why feelings of sadness and hopelessness commonly occur when you deal with family problems
- What fundamental confusion accounts for many failed adult relationships
- Why is love something you do rather than something you feel
- Why romantic love is not the most critical element in a long-term marriage
- What you need to do when great passion is replaced by familiarity or apathy
- How to know if your love relationship is codependent
- Why more feelings are expressed in a destructive, negative manner within the family than in any other place

. . . and more!

Also by Susanna McMahon

The Portable Problem Solver:
Coping with Life's Stressors

The Portable Therapist

The Portable
Problem Solver

Having Healthy Relationships

Susanna McMahon, Ph.D.

A Dell Trade Paperback

A DELL TRADE PAPERBACK

Published by
Dell Publishing
a division of
Bantam Doubleday Dell Publishing Group, Inc.
1540 Broadway
New York, New York 10036

Library of Congress Cataloging-in-Publication Data
McMahon, Susanna.
    The portable problem solver : having healthy relationships / by
Susanna McMahon.
      p.   cm.
    ISBN 0-440-50734-0
    1. Interpersonal relations.   2. Problem solving.   3. Self-help
techniques.   I. Title.
HM132.M3745 1996
158′.2—dc20   95-26218
                                                        CIP

Printed in the United States of America

Published simultaneously in Canada

August 1996

10 9 8 7 6 5 4 3 2 1

BVG

To my mother, who began the process—
To my daughters, who continually refine it—
For these teachers of my lifetime, with love.

All great problems call for great love.
                    —F. W. NIETZSCHE

*(Problem Solvers): What they once perceived as problems
they now perceive as opportunities.*
                    —M. SCOTT PECK

∽ Contents

∽ Acknowledgments

There are so many people to thank, especially when dealing with this type of book, because the memories, the experiences, and the joy of having relationships, along with the pain and difficulties, exist through the people I know and love. I will begin with my mother, Joan Quarm, for being Mother and for raising me with love; she is also a great editor and she vastly improved this book. Next I need to thank my four brothers, Michael, Robin, Chris, and Nick, for teaching me about life and men; together we coped, yelled, and laughed through all the hard times. All my experience has taught me to realize how very much I respect, value, and appreciate my husband, Timothy. My daughters, Jennifer and Catherine, and my stepdaughter, Kelly, are three of the most intense joys of my life, and at times the greatest challenges. I thank them for teaching me that healthy relationships with family members are always about process and development. I especially want to acknowledge Jennifer for her meticulous comments about this book.

Our adopted family in Germany, Dr. and Mrs. Ernst Scharizer, Beatrice and Reinhard Walter, allowed Tim and me the experience of family in another culture; we love and appreciate what they have given us. Friends are critical components for a balanced life, and I am fortunate to know some wonderful ones. In Europe: Elizabeth, Judy, Alf and Betty, Anne and Jesus, Carol and Klaus; in the States: Art and Janet, Gloria and Buzz, Eldon and Marge, Beth and Paul, Barbara and Rusty, Joyce and Andy, Carolyn and Jim. All of these have shared their homes and hearts with us. Thank you all, and all my other treasured friends.

There are two adolescent friends of mine who were incredibly helpful by sharing their thoughts and perceptions about this difficult stage of development. I thank Anne Genung from Dallas and Sam West from Michigan for being so open, supportive, and honest.

Everything that I have learned has been reinforced and intensified by knowing my clients. Without you I could not be either a clinician or an author; I certainly would never have had the courage to tackle such difficult topics without your inspiration. Please know that I have thought about all of you with great love and admiration as I wrote these pages.

And last, but never least, I want to thank my agent, Margret McBride, and my editors at Dell, Trish Todd and Eric Wybenga. They are the best and I thank them for their support.

↝ Introduction

You cannot live without relationships. You cannot *not* relate. All human beings involve themselves with others. From simply nodding and smiling at strangers through intensely intimate and life-affirming interactions, you spend most of your life relating in varying degrees with others. The time not spent with another becomes the time you spend relating with yourself. Therefore it makes complete sense that your relationships and your problems are inseparable. Relationships begin with those people you need in order to survive, and they continue with those who enhance the quality of your life. Because they are fundamental to life, the problems they create can be the most challenging or devastating ones that you will enounter.

Every day presents a new challenge because you are going to encounter problems, you are not going to have your needs met in the way you want them to be met, and you are going to have to resolve these issues with either the aid or the hindrance of others. It is no wonder that you will often feel overwhelmed, and at times even helpless or hopeless. Because relationships are so essential, the difficulties you have with them can often seem greater than your capacity to deal with them. You add to your discomfort when you hold the illusions that life should be problem-free and that your relationships should always be conflict-free.

You have been trained by parents, teachers, peers, and the media to believe that you need to be happy and that being with others should function to further your happiness. You have been fed an illusory ideal of perfect relationships, beginning with an unrealistic model of family life and continuing with society's delusional image of perfect relationships with lovers, children, friends, and co-workers. Surely you have watched movies with happy endings that result from the characters discovering love. Most likely, you have been taught to seek those who love you and to shun those who do not. You have been lied to and led down the dangerous road of impossible expectations. But you probably continue to love the fantasy and to seek it in your own life. When you do so, you will tend to perceive your problems as being in the way or as inconvenient hurdles that prevent you from living a healthy and productive life. What you have not been taught are two simple realities: Life is a problem, and all relationships are difficult. Learning to deal with these realities becomes your personal challenge and provides your opportunities for self-development.

Accepting these realities stops the resentments and frustrations that occur when you are aspiring to an ideal that is in actuality an impossible fantasy. The acceptance that problematic relationships are part of your life and that problems *are* life may be too painful for you to bear unless you can also realize that humans are masterful problem solvers. All the things that you have and that you have learned, all your relationships, good and bad, all your attributes and skills, have brought you to this place and time where you now live. Everything that has happened to you is now part of who you are at this moment. Your present skills were developed from your past difficulties and are directed toward solving current and future problems. Without these difficulties there would be no challenges, and without challenges there would be no growth. Without growth there is no life.

Relationships provide the first and most important arena in which to learn problem-solving skills. They allow you to learn to love and they reward you when you are loved in return. They teach you to share, to communicate, to appreciate, and to belong. But they are not always about being comfortable, safe, and happy. Yes, you can have great happiness and joy with those you care about, but that is not the primary function of relationships. They simply cannot do for you what you are unwilling or unable to do for yourself. You cannot exist without them, but you also cannot make them the reasons for your existence. All relationships are temporary—they always end in some way—and all involve change. Healthy relationships recognize this time limitation and do not place impossible expectations upon others. In order to have healthy relationships, you must first be healthy yourself. One attribute of being healthy is recognizing that your problems teach you to be an effective problem solver, that all problems are challenges, and that all your difficulties lead you to the discovery of the best within yourself.

In my first book, *The Portable Therapist,* the concepts of weak ego (esteem received from external sources) and self-esteem (worth and love of the Self) were presented in the context of therapy issues. These concepts are further developed throughout this book with respect to how they impact upon your relationships. All problems, including those pertaining to relationships, have a basic core: insecurity. When you are insecure, you are unable to take care of yourself and consequently will feel the need to attach to others in order to try to feel more secure. These attachments, initially designed to provide security and vanquish your fears, end up by constraining you and making your life more difficult. Thus there is a direct correlation between your problems with others and the amount to which you are attached to them. The more you need others in order to feel secure, the more dependent you become upon them, and this dependency always creates difficulties. Expecting others to fulfill your needs means you cannot let go and let be. These are probably the most difficult things you will ever learn to do because they mean you have given up your unrealistic expectations and impossible illusions and are able to satisfy your own needs. Paradoxically they are also the only things you can do to ultimately resolve your problems. Letting go and allowing others to be can only be achieved when you feel secure enough to detach and take care of yourself, emotionally and physically.

Before you can begin the detachment process, you must first work through and understand the lessons your problems teach you. In this book seven steps are listed after each specific relationship topic, which, hopefully, will provide you with concrete, practical, and specific activities to help you deal with your problems. These steps are a guide and are designed to point out possible resolutions. The seven steps represent the process of becoming a problem solver and they are sequential because the early steps are the foundation for the later ones. How you use them will vary depending upon where you are in the detachment process with each specific relationship problem.

It is important, however, to realize that what you do to solve your problem of the moment is not nearly as important as how you perceive yourself while you are being challenged by your difficulties. This focus on self-perception becomes most relevant when you encounter the problems that cannot be fixed, the ones that can only be accepted. You will not be able to accept that some problems are insoluble unless you can first accept your own imperfections. You cannot become unattached from others until you first learn to be secure within yourself. Thus your problems serve to point out where you need to work on your own security. In this problem-solving process called life you will become hopeless, negative, discouraged, and discouraging unless you first learn to love yourself. Then you will be able to believe in your own goodness and worth, recognize that you can only live in the moment, create your own hope, encourage yourself, support others, and face your difficulties. You will be able to do so not with fear and anxiety but with awareness of your incredible problem-solving skills and abilities. Your problems function as personal guides and teach you about yourself; your relationships do the same. It may help you to know that we are all fellow students in this process and that none of us is ever completely alone.

Because relationship problems are so pervasive and encompassing, I have divided this book into nine sections, each dealing with a specific type of relationship. The first one is the family you are born to and raised in, the original family. This family teaches you how to relate with others and sets the pattern for your future relationships. The next area is your love relationships, not because they occur chronologically in your life but because of the impact they have on your life satisfaction. Sex and sexuality follow, as they are a critical component of love relationships. Then comes the chosen family, your spouse and your own children, followed by separation and divorce and the problems they incur. The sixth area for relationship problems deals with friends, and the seventh covers colleagues and co-workers. The next area for discussion, and usually the one that is most overlooked and yet most critical of all, is the relationship you have with your Self. The final area deals with the community and how your belief and value systems impact upon your worldview.

I wrote this book to try to make sense of relationships and the continual difficulties they bring to life. There are very few references, but this does not mean they do not exist. Every paragraph brings to mind someone who taught me or something I learned. Every concept in this book is founded in theory or practice or experience. If the ideas presented sound familiar to you, it is because many of them have been around a long time. If they sound controversial, I take full responsibility. This book was conceived from my problems, mistakes, and failures. It was nurtured by my experiences with others and by the discovery that we share the same difficulties. It grew from my conviction that there must be something right, appropriate, even necessary, in having all these relationship challenges. It came into being when I recognized the virtue of becoming a problem solver.

Because I can only write what I know, what I have learned and experienced for myself or through others, I am constantly being forced to confront my own limitations. As you probably know, this is always painful. Writing this book was often painful. But there is profit from the pain. I grew as I wrote; I hope you will also grow as you read. If so, the pain will have been well worth the reward. This book is a psychospiritual journey because it begins with the psychology of relationships and ends with the spirituality you develop through them.

1 ᴄ *The Original Family*

The Very Beginning

Imagine that you are once again a newborn. What do you want? What are your needs? You have recently left a place of great safety; perhaps you will never know such safety again. You have left a place where all your physical needs were satisfied even before you were aware of what you needed. You have entered an unfamiliar and often hostile world, with bright lights to hurt your eyes, loud noises to hurt your ears, painful cramps when your stomach is empty or when you have gas, and large, very large, objects that stare at you, make funny noises at you, and sometimes jerk you around. You have discovered pain and you are not even one hour old. But along with pain you have also discovered great comfort. When this large object holds you and you hear and feel another heart beating, when you suck on the thing thrust into your tiny mouth, when you are rocked gently and patted, you feel incredible comfort—probably more comfort and contentment than you experienced in the womb. For that safe place was sometimes lonely, and the only comfort you had then was your thumb. As an unborn infant you cried, felt lonely, and desired something unknown to you. Now, after birth, in the midst of all this pain, there is exquisite comfort when you are held and fed and loved. You have found your desire to be caressed. You are no longer lonely. You are getting affection, which is as necessary as food for survival.

Thus begins your lifetime trade-off with relationships: You will experience pain in order to get the comfort. You will risk being hurt in order not to be lonely. You exchange great safety for danger mixed with moments of pleasure. You are born in order to experience humanity, and being human means experiencing pain and pleasure, which are not in your control.

The First Relationship

After a short time you discover that some of the large objects around you are *your* objects. They seem to be there much of the time, and to feed you and pick you up when you cry. They go crazy when you smile at them and sometimes make noises that soothe you and make you feel safe. Now, if only you can get them to make you feel safe all the time, you will have it all—the safety you lost along with the comfort you now crave, without the pain. You have begun your first relationship! You know what you want; now, how to get the other person to give it to you? This other person, you learn, is called Mother and when she gives you what you want and need, you are happy. But when she does not, you are miserable. And worse yet, as time goes by, you start becoming afraid that she will not be there for you and you will be abandoned. If this happens, you fear that you will not be able to survive. You have become attached and you are developing normally.

Making sure that Mother is there becomes your first critical priority. Because she means a lessening of pain and a provision of comfort, keeping Mother happy and attentive to you becomes your first problem. And early on you start trying to figure out what will make someone else (Mother) happy so that you can get your needs met. You soon discover that sometimes what you do works, but that sometimes doing the same thing—smiling, gurgling, hugging—does not work. Now what to do? You will have to learn new tricks, new things to do, in order to keep Mother interested in you and coming back to fill your needs and wants.

Manipulation

Trying to figure out what others want and behaving accordingly begins very early and sets the pattern for all future relationships. *Manipulation* simply means doing something in order to get something. It is not "bad," because it is a necessary part of the human process. *Manipulation* is another word for control, and we all begin life by trying to control. It may be unconscious, as in the case of the infant crying to be held or fed, or it may be conscious, as in the case of the toddler putting up his arms to be picked up, but it is all trying to control, or manipulating. Babies will naturally play one parent against the other by seeming to favor one more, and will sometimes exhibit jealousy of the marital relationship. They clearly express their preferences; sometimes they want only Mother and other times only Father will satisfy them. There is no human being who has not used manipulation or who has not been manipulated. This is an important reality of all relationships—they involve manipulation. This only becomes a problem when it is denied, developed as a specific style of relating, or consciously utilized to hurt or take advantage of the other.

The Importance of Love

Our first relationship is with the mother, or mother figure, and it becomes the first arena of conflict in our lives. It is no wonder that so much therapeutic attention has been given to this primary relationship. Infants initially perceive the mother as part of themselves; later on they recognize there is separation. Even so, Mother is critical for our survival and the way we first feel about ourselves. If Mother loves us, we begin life with the idea that we are lovable. When she does not love us, we begin life by believing that there is something wrong with us, that we are defective and unlovable. But suppose, in reality, that there is something wrong with Mother? Suppose it is her defect, her fault, that she does not love us? Unfortunately it takes many years before the young child can even begin to entertain this concept, and in those intermittent years a great deal of damage can be inflicted upon the unloved child.

It is important to know that it is *never* the child's fault for not being loved. It is *always* the responsibility of the mother or primary caretaker to give love to the child. *All* children are lovable. All of us, including you, come into the world ready to love and be loved, wanting to play and to be held and to give and receive joy from this crazy world. When love does not come our way, it is never because we do not deserve it. Even the most difficult infant, toddler, or young child is lovable. When it comes to love, there is no such thing as a defective child. There is, however, such a thing as a defective parent, and unfortunately there are too many of these around. If Mother is incapable of love, then we can be saved by Father loving us or, if not a parent, any loving caretaker will in some ways compensate. It is essential to feel loved early on in our lives. The knowledge that somebody loves us for who we are is vital for helping us cope and for teaching us that we have worthy identities. The completely unloved child can be more handicapped and disabled than the physically or mentally disabled one. Unfortunately the child cannot know any of this yet.

Taking the Blame

One of our earliest problems in the primary relationship occurs with the attribution of defect. The child often tends to feel overly responsible and to internalize external situations. He (or she) takes the blame for things out of his control and therefore not within his power to change, thereby leaving himself open to victimization. The child of abusive parents tends to feel that he is the reason for the abuse. Often he believes that if only he can be good enough, or never "bad," the abuse will stop. Frequently, by taking responsibility for adult behavior he leaves the parents free to scapegoat and victimize him. In so doing, the child has become part of a dysfunctional family—a family that does not work in a constructive and safe manner for its members. He has exchanged safety for danger, without the comfort that makes such a trade worthwhile.

A great deal of attention has recently been directed toward the dysfunctional family. There are large numbers of adults who are trying to deal with unresolved childhood issues. One of the main reasons that childhood can be problematic for the adult stems from this assumption that children are responsible for the parents' defects. One reality of childhood is that children become victims because they are small, helpless, and dependent. Unfortunately most of us do not realize or recognize this until we become adults. Instead, as we were growing up, many of us thought that we caused the problems or miseries within our families. As children we perceived the world through egocentric eyes and therefore could not separate ourselves from the family. We had not yet learned to be objective and to understand that we may have had little or nothing to do with the underlying causes of the familial dysfunction.

Certainly this lack of responsibility is very clear when we are the child of an alcoholic or abusive parent. It is also true, to some degree, for all children of all parents. Our parents may do terrible things to us, sometimes inadvertently, but when we are little, we need them and will work hard to love and be loved by them. Therefore we will frequently take the blame for problems; in doing so we create an illusion of having some control and keep alive a hope for change. When we blamed the problem on our "not being good enough" and tried to become better in order to solve the problem or change the family dynamics, we were trying to have some control over the situation. If we had felt completely helpless to affect change, we would probably have lost all hope that change would ever occur. When we do not have control, and yet are dependent upon those who do, the assumption of responsibility can function to foster an illusion of control.

Asserting Identity

Even in the most loving home, with parents who take responsibility for their actions, conflict occurs when the toddler begins to assert identity. By two years of age he (or she) wants things that the parent will not give. He may want to stay up all night or to cross the street by himself, or run freely. The two-year-old wants to touch things that may hurt him and is constantly testing those around him. There is no way that conflict can be avoided. This child, in order to grow, learn, and develop normally, has to be "difficult" as part of the process of discovering a separate identity from the parents. He has now engaged in another trade-off: being "good," which means doing what the parent wants and likes and thereby getting rewarded, versus being "bad," which means receiving disapproval, but asserting his personality and discovering important boundaries. This can become a lose-lose situation for the child who desperately needs approval but also developmentally needs to learn and grow by challenging the system. Thus a third major problem surfaces—

that of doing what you want, no matter the consequences, versus doing what others expect in order to gain their approval, affection, and positive rewards.

Three of the major problems that occur in relationships have already surfaced, and the child is only two! He has encountered the problem of trying to figure out what will make another happy, taken responsibility without having control, and discovered that what he wants may cause negative consequences.

Controlling Feelings

This situation becomes compounded as the child begins to verbalize feelings. It is normal and healthy to feel sad, angry, lonely, and confused. It is also developmentally appropriate to try to use feelings to gain power. The child may try having temper tantrums or screaming to test their effectiveness in controlling the parent. However, most parents do not understand this process and will either overreact or give in to the child. Parents themselves generally have difficulty with negative feelings, and they try to train the child by punishing him when such feelings are expressed. Their child, who is an excellent student of human nature, quickly learns that negative feelings often lead to adverse consequences, while positive feelings—happiness, contentment, satisfaction, appreciation—generate positive rewards. Often feelings are labeled. It is "good" to feel happy and secure and "bad" to feel angry, sad, or confused. Because the child wants to be perceived as good, he will try to control his feelings. It takes many years and great maturity to learn that feelings cannot be controlled. The ability to feel is the major component of being human; therefore feelings are not good or bad; they just are.

Understanding this helps to make sense of the familiar process in which children try to control their negative feelings in order to please their parents. Feelings will be hidden or denied, thereby causing frustration, lack of control, and eventual dissociation from all feeling. Because we cannot block negative feelings without also blocking positive ones, this process of dissociation leads to self-alienation and lack of self-awareness. When this occurs, intimacy is impossible. Intimacy can be defined as the awareness of our feelings as they occur and the safety to express them to another. How can we be intimate with others when we have lost the ability to be so with ourselves?

Learning Roles

As the child continues to grow and expand his repertoire of relationships, problems seem to expand as well. Most children have siblings to deal with, along with grandparents, aunts, uncles, and cousins. The role of the individual now becomes an issue. While the only child may have the clearest role—that of "the child"—he must also assume more responsibility for satisfying parents' expectations. Frequently he may become the focus of too much attention, and be forced into becoming a pseudoadult and losing his valuable childhood. The child with siblings does not have an easier situation; it is just different. There is no ideal role to play. The first child is similar to the only child in that the roles predispose both to become over-achievers and skilled people pleasers. The oldest child has the parents' undivided attention for a while and quickly learns how to work for rewards. This process of being perhaps too finely tuned in to what other people are thinking and feeling tends to be replayed in all future relationships.

Middle children often report having difficulties with their identities because their role may seem nebulous and uncertain. They often feel that they become lost in the family dynamics and do not seem to have as clearly defined a place in the family as do the first and last children. This middle child may feel that he is either too old or too young in comparison to his siblings. He may carry this sense of unclear identity and lack of belonging with him into the future.

The last child, the baby, tends to adopt the role of having less responsibility and being allowed to remain immature and needy. Typically the youngest is rewarded by the family for his dependency and will carry this neediness into other relationships. He will not view this role as easier than the others and will often express regret that he can never "catch up" or be perceived as mature and capable. Within his family he will always be considered the "baby." Usually this is the child with the fewest photographs and the least amount of attention for achieving developmental milestones.

By an early age children have learned that it is not enough to be what they are; they must live up to expectations determined by their birth order and by their role in the family system. And they have discovered that these expectations and roles, by their very nature, are limiting and difficult to maintain. The problem of being has now reared its ugly head and the questions Who am I? and What am I? become relevant. It is no wonder the child is confused. At this point he is incapable of sorting through or solving any of these difficulties. He has not yet matured and learned to be objective about his roles or to recognize that these limitations are external ones and not the reality of his internal self.

Developing an Identity

It may help to remember that all these problems are normal in that they are part of the developmental process called living. There is no way to avoid them, and there is no reason to try to prevent them from occurring. We need them, we need to be challenged by them, and we need to work through them, in order to become well-rounded, balanced, whole human beings. All of us have encountered these conflicts to some degree; we can benefit from them if they serve to teach us about ourselves. Functional families are rare, and even when they do exist, and we were lucky enough to have been raised in one, we will still have encountered the foregoing difficulties. Our own family may have been functional (most are not), but the world certainly is not, because it does not work for and with us. If we were fortunate as children to have been loved and cared for, protected and stimulated, encouraged and positively reinforced, we were still not free from danger because we could not remain in the cocoon of a loving family, but were forced to interact with the rest of the world.

Fighting the Battle

Childhood is a war zone. As soon as the child marches out into the world, he discovers that there is an undeclared battle going on out there. This battle, as is true of all wars, is about power and control, the strong subsuming the weak. The child must fight for identity, rights, property, and feelings, and soon discovers that life is not fair and that bullies all too often win. This war called childhood uses subtle weapons—lies, name-calling, false accusations, rejection—along with aggressive ones—hitting, shoving, beating up, and other physical abuse. How many adults, on a daily basis, are pushed around physically, called hurtful names, and frightened by those who are bigger and stronger? And when they are, adults are labeled battered. Children are rarely thought of as such when the wounds are inflicted by other children.

Group Safety

Children quickly learn all about their own weaknesses; others constantly remind them of their defects. They know all about loneliness, rejection, pain, unfairness, helplessness, and the importance of belonging with someone else. In order to survive, they form alliances, develop power through strength in numbers, and learn to be rejecting, hurtful, and mean to outsiders. This may help to account for the current trend toward belonging to a gang. And so another problem of relationships has developed: How much of ourselves and our own feelings do we give up in order to belong to the powerful group? We learn to hate, to lie, to hurt, to change our own values and feelings in order to belong, for belonging means safety, and safety demands a high price. As is true of any soldier in any war, our own individual needs, principles, and desires must be in line with those of the larger group in order to win, and we must change ourselves in order to have cohesion and be a part of the group.

Another conflict often occurs when the norms and values of the peer group do not agree with those of the family. By the age of nine, and sometimes earlier, the child must choose between parents and peers. In our culture the older child most often chooses peers and exacerbates the difficulties with the family. Going along with the group leads to more rewards and reinforcements than going along with parents and family. The child spends more time with peers, and status in the world—the status that counts—is determined by the peer group. It seems logical, then, that the child belongs to the family, agrees and believes in the family's mores and values, before the age of nine and after the age of twenty. This is not always the case, but it is generally true. From nine through twenty the child belongs to the significant peer group.

The Conflict of Adolescence

If childhood is a war zone, then adolescence is face-to-face conflict. And the enemy is most often the family of origin. There is a small parallel here between our most recent types of wars and personal developmental progress. Before puberty most children are engaged in a war, which in one way can be compared to World War II. They go off to the school environment, learn to do battle, but return to a loving home that provides support, security, and safety. This child is a hero when he does well and is nurtured when he loses. The family is perceived as "on his side" and "fighting for him." The family is much like America during World War II: We knew what we were fighting for and we respected our soldiers for being there. They had a job to do and we stood behind them and honored their fight.

Adolescence changes the war; the battlegrounds are not clearly defined and the family is frequently defined as the enemy. This is similar to what happened in America during the Vietnam era. No one is clearly prepared for this conflict; no one is really sure what he is fighting for. The rules change frequently and no one seems to want to be involved. The adolescent, with very few exceptions, is not emotionally capable or mature enough to make sense of it. Unfortunately neither are most parents. "Dirty" fighting, breaking all the rules, and being constantly surprised and unsupported seem to be the nature of this conflict. If words were actual weapons, no one today would survive adolescence. We would all blow each other away.

The comparison of the Vietnam veteran with the adolescent may help us understand what adolescence is about. First of all it is a traumatic time and the trauma is not clearly defined. There is no common enemy and the reasons for the conflict are not clear. The Vietnam vet knew that he had to do whatever he could in order to survive; the adolescent also feels he is doing whatever he has to in order to assert his identity. He is fighting for psychic survival. The family, like the country, is no longer perceived as supportive and nurturing. The parents are confused by this alien in their midst; the adolescent knows that he no longer belongs, in the comfort sense, to the family, and he feels he must fight outside them and within them. There seems to be no place of refuge except among the peer group. For some unfortunates there is not even the peer group to support them. The Vietnam veteran who could not make the transition back to a hostile country developed symptoms called post-traumatic stress disorder (PTSD). This meant they were stuck in the trauma and unable to reintegrate back into normal life. Perhaps those who cannot transition from adolescence into adulthood are analogous to the Vietnam veteran with PTSD.

Teenage Stress

Adolescence cannot be clinically defined as a post-traumatic stress disorder because it is a normal developmental stage and therefore is not outside the range of usual experience. Also the symptoms usually disappear around the age of twenty. However, some of the prevalent symptoms of PTSD do occur in adolescence, and the comparison may be helpful for understanding what the adolescent is going through. While he does not experience the recurrence of trauma (flashbacks), which is a critical component of the disorder, he frequently experiences a numbing of general responsiveness and an avoidance of difficult stimuli. These manifest themselves as efforts to avoid thoughts or emotions, feelings of detachment or estrangement from others, restricted affect (inability to express feelings), hopelessness at times about the future, and diminished interest in significant activities, particularly those involving the family. To the adolescent these symptoms are sporadic; to the true PTSD victim they are chronic. Irritability, outbursts of anger, and intermittent thoughts that the world is out to get them are familiar traits. Here the similarities end, as the Vietnam vet, the PTSD victim, has to deal with trauma outside normal human experience, whereas the adolescent is dealing with an entirely normal experience—his own developmental growth.

Problems Are Development

By trying to solve some types of problems, we often create others. Yet many of these conflicts may lead to positive long-term results. If these issues—the problems of identity, belongingness, expression of feelings, rejection of others' values, assertion of the self, and experimentation with many types of relationships—are dealt with in adolescence, when they are developmentally appropriate and part of the maturation process, they will not need to resurface continually in the same ways. In other words the work we do in adolescence paves the way for different work to be done in adulthood. The problems we experience and resolve during this period form the foundation on which we can build for the rest of our lives. We cannot develop an identity without questioning it. We cannot have meaningful relationships unless we experiment and test them. We cannot become mature until we have first been immature. Thus adolescence is a necessary conflict. It leads to the development of the very life that the adolescent is challenging. If the challenge is great and painful and difficult, then the results from the learning experience may also be great and meaningful and valuable.

As stated, relationships are about learning. They involve pain and discomfort, rejection and acceptance. During the twenty or so years of intimate attachment to the family of origin, the child and later the adolescent have encountered all major problems associated with relationships. The infant learned the problems of exchanging safety for danger plus pleasure, and experienced having pain and comfort instead of safety. The infant also learned manipulation (getting what you want from others) as well as trying to please others so that they will fulfill one's needs. The young child discovered the problem of taking responsibility without having control, and the danger of internalizing an external situation. Power, exemplified by the urge to control others, has been tried and tested. This school-age child has also learned that conflict is unavoidable and that there is a price to pay in trying to please others at one's own expense. He (or she) has learned that there is a conflict between developing his own identity (doing what he wants) and pleasing others (doing what they want).

The issue of being good versus doing wrong has already surfaced, along with the difficulty of intimacy—being able to express feelings in safety. As the child has grown, expectations and roles have also grown. The basic existential problems of being— Who am I? and What am I?—are already present, as are lifetime conflicts concerning power and control issues. The school-age child has dealt with the problem of how much to give up in order to belong to the group. Puberty brings the additional problems of identity, rule breaking, and unclear conflict, which are exacerbated during adolescence. The problems of rejecting and being rejected, changing mind and mood quickly, being overly concerned with *me,* and searching for good relationships, ones that work, all develop during adolescence. All these conflicts will be replayed and reworked and rehashed in different arenas as we continue to grow and develop throughout our lives.

Stuck in Old Patterns

These problems are developmentally appropriate if they help us move on. If, by having them, we learn, grow, mature, and become adults, then they have worked for us; they have functioned as an important part of development. But suppose that we have gotten stuck. For whatever reasons, we have not learned from these problems, but are merely repeating them in our present life. We are still replaying our dependencies, rehashing our old feelings, reworking manipulations, and responding only to our own needs. We are living a script and following our old patterns. This results in immature functioning, living emotionally as if we are still within our first environment, and at best only masquerading as adults. How can we get past this original family and grow up? To begin the process of becoming unstuck, we can follow the steps that follow in the next chapter for problem-solving the family of origin. Even if we are relatively mature and secure in our relationships with this family, it will be constructive to go through each step to see if there is anything residual still affecting us. Most of us will find that it is a lifelong process to problem-solve our beginnings. Do not despair over the amount of time that may have to be spent, because the rewards gained from each small step are incredible and well worth a lifetime's work. Remember, it is all process. In life there is no completion and no perfection.

II ⌒ Problem-Solving the Original Family

1. Accepting

Look at your family with adult eyes, instead of through the eyes of the child. See it objectively. Forget your illusions and desires about family. Imagine that each member of your family is a stranger, and describe each one to someone you trust. If you can do this, you will soon see that each is imperfect. There are some good things about all of them, but there are also some traits you hate. Use your clinical eyes and you will see that they are as insecure in their own ways as you are in yours. Each member has a dark side, a side that he (or she) does not like to show or discuss, a side that is trying to cover up the fears and loss of control.

It is important to recognize that you know the dark sides of your family members much better than you know your own. Accept what you know and see. It is futile and frustrating to try to change the dark sides of others; it is also a waste of time to deny that they exist. See them and accept them. The things you like and dislike about them are your reality of what your family is to you. Recognize that you do not have all the data and that you will never know what created their weaknesses. Also know that your perceptions are dependent upon your own dark side. Acceptance is not understanding. Acceptance is not change. It is simply seeing and allowing. Acceptance is also not agreement. You do not have to like or condone what you are seeing. You do, however, for your own health, have to accept what you see as the reality of what is. Perception is reality to the perceiver. Acceptance helps to keep your perceptions clean.

Above all, accept the fact that you are good. You do not have to work at "being good" because you already have that goodness within yourself. No matter what has happened to you in your family, no matter how awful, you are still good. The hard work is living your goodness; children will do this more naturally when they are loved and nurtured. Even if you missed out on family nurturance, it is never too late. Nurture yourself. This is easier to do if you accept that you are worthy. And you are!

2. Letting Go

If you have recognized that you are still carrying around destructive patterns of relating, due to early training and experiences, do not despair. The one great thing about learned behavior is that it can be un-learned, or changed. Patterns of behavior are learned; they are not fixed—they are not your personality. The most critical realization in changing the influence of family training occurs when you recognize that your needs as an adult are quite different from your needs as a child. You are no longer dependent upon your parents for survival. You can make it in this world without them. This is no small realization, for it leads to the idea that you can begin to perceive your family through different eyes than the ones you had in your earlier life. If you can exist without your parents (and you can!), then you are no longer dependent upon them for approval. As a child you equated approval with survival; your parents would not abandon you if they loved (approved of) you. As an adult you can survive, no matter what your parent thinks or feels. Let go of your need for approval. You can make it, you are free!

All this may sound simplistic, especially for those who have progressed past the need for parental approval. You might be surprised to discover that most people carry around a huge need to recapture that early approval, to be the ideal child, to be loved and approved of unconditionally. If you did not get this from your family, you probably tried to find parental substitutes in other relationships, in order to satisfy these needs.

Let go of any idea that you were or are responsible for the dysfunction in your family. You were also not to blame for any trauma or pain that was inflicted upon you. Remember, you are only responsible for what you can control, and as a child you could control very little. What you may have thought you could control, what you may have blamed yourself for all these years, is probably an illusion of control based on your need to change the situation. Now that you can change the situation, now that you do have some control and you are no longer vulnerable and dependent, let go of your dangerous illusions and unrealistic expectations.

In the last decade a great deal of therapeutic intervention has been aimed at the inner child. All of us carry around a small child within us—one who remembers the fear of abandonment, who feels rejected and unloved, or only conditionally loved. This inner child is seeking whatever it missed in its development. It is desperately crying out to remedy any unfulfilled needs. Your family, your parents, cannot fulfill these needs, for whatever reasons. But you can! Stop worrying about what your parents did not do and begin parenting your own inner child. If you need approval, give yourself approval. Whatever you may want your parents to say or do, say or do to yourself. Keep saying and doing positive things to yourself until you believe them. Then, and only then, will you be free from your early needs to receive approval from others. Remember, it feels good to have others approve of you; it is pleasant, but it is not necessary. It is necessary, however, to approve of yourself. It is impossible to learn to let go of the need for others' approval without self-approval. It is also impossible to let others be without letting yourself be, and this means taking care of your own needs and allowing others to do the same.

3. Expressing Feelings

Once you can accept your family and let go of needing them, you will most likely discover that you have powerful feelings hidden inside. If you do, you will undoubtedly find anger and sadness. The anger is natural and to be expected because you entered this world as a helpless but hopeful little creature and your family repeatedly hurt you, misunderstood you, and inflicted pain upon you. Your anger, in a sense, defines you. It has been there for many years, and until it is actively expressed, it will stay with you. Unfortunately this unreleased anger, understandable as it is, will also weigh you down and create many unnecessary problems. It must be acknowledged, expressed, and let go of in order for you to be whole, balanced, and emotionally healthy. Old anger is like rot; it is pervasive and it destroys whatever it encounters. Get that anger out. You do not have to confront the ones you are angry with in order to release it. You do not have to explode or be afraid of it. Simply acknowledging and expressing the emotion will allow it to be released. There are several techniques for expressing anger in a constructive manner. A good one is the letter-writing exercise: Write a letter, or several letters, that you will *never* send, to each of your parents or to your siblings. Write to the person in your family who has hurt you the most and with whom you are still angry. Write how you feel and why you feel this way. Keep writing until you can actually feel the anger dissipate. You will know when it is gone—there will be nothing left to write.

Do not be afraid of your anger. If it overwhelms you, ask for help. Get a therapist to work with you on this issue. Join a support group. Share your feelings with a close and trusted friend, someone who is sensible and able to empathize with you. Talk about whatever you are feeling and thinking, but do not act on these feelings. Talking and writing about your anger are constructive; acting on it can be very destructive. Do not try to inflict pain on anyone else because you are angry. Go for the release and not the revenge.

Another effective technique is to beat up your pillow as you imagine it to be the object of your anger. Beat it as much as you need to until, again, you feel the release. You can also use a punching bag or throw tennis balls against a wall or tear pieces of paper into small fragments as you imagine tearing into the one you are angry with. Your anger will dissipate; it only needs to be expressed in order to be released.

Feelings of sadness and hopelessness are also frequent when you deal with family issues. These feelings can be overwhelming and lead to long-term depression, unless they, too, can be expressed and released. Again, ask for help. Make sure that you are being supported and nurtured when you express your feelings of loss. Cry, remember how hurt and lost you felt, and cry some more. Cry for your lost hopes, your unfulfilled dreams, your undeserved pain, your lack of attention, your innocence and vulnerability. Cry for your lost child, your lost self. Cry until there are no more tears to cry. Again, you will feel it when you have released your sadness. You will be able to let go.

Express all the feelings that you may have when you think back to your childhood. Try not to analyze or justify or rationalize them. They do not belong to your head; they belong in your heart. Having them is the important issue, having them, expressing them, and letting go of them. Remember, your feelings are not right or wrong, good or bad, worthy or unworthy. They are what they are and you cannot control them. You can only experience them, express them, and let them move on. You need to be free of old feelings in order to have new ones. Unexpressed, feelings linger and contaminate the reality of the present moment. Expressed feelings that are acknowledged become released feelings. Then, and only then, are you free and able to live in the present.

4. Taking Responsibility

When you think about your family with an objective mind, you will be able to perceive what things were in your control and what things were not. As a child very little was actually in your control, and you cannot take responsibility for things that were not. During the first decade of life your parents or caretakers had almost total control over you. The responsibility rests with them. If you were labeled "bad," chances are it was not your fault. What you may previously have considered your fault was probably your response to unfulfilled needs or a dysfunctional system. Children will frequently act as scapegoats to sick family patterns. Do not take responsibility for things that were not your fault. Try to discover the relationship between your "bad" behavior and what was going on in your family. They are correlated.

To some degree the above is also true for the period of adolescence. However, because the parents and family had less control during this second decade of life, they also had less responsibility for you. Take responsibility for the actions that you had control over. You may find it necessary to share the responsibility with your family, but do take whatever responsibility you can. Try not to play the blame game and also try to avoid justifying your actions. You will only end up by feeling little or no control over yourself or your life. It is much simpler, cleaner, and more realistic to take responsibility only when it is yours and then to get on with the next step.

5. Forgiving

Whatever you have taken responsibility for, now forgive yourself for doing. That's right, forgive yourself. No matter what it is, no matter how awful or destructive or negative, forgive yourself. You cannot go back and do it differently, you cannot change your past, in many cases you cannot even make amends. The only thing left for you to actively do about your past is to forgive. Forgive yourself before you forgive your parents, but only forgive yourself for what was your fault, your responsibility because it was in your control. You cannot forgive yourself for something that was not your mistake.

Forgiving yourself may sound easy but, when done correctly, is difficult, because forgiving always implies blaming. You can only forgive what you know to be wrong or bad behavior. Forgive yourself for being wrong—you have been, lots of times. Forgive yourself for doing "bad" things; you are human and therefore have erred and behaved badly. But do not forgive yourself for being a bad person, because you are not a bad person and you were not a bad child. Doing something "bad" is not being bad.

After you have forgiven yourself, then you can forgive your parents and siblings. Forgive them for being imperfect, for not taking care of you in the ways that you wanted them to, for being mean and hurtful and insensitive. Forgive them for the pain they inflicted upon you. It helps to do this if you can realize that they were trying their best, given their insecurities and weaknesses. You can only forgive others when you have worked through the previous steps. Forgiveness is dependent upon acceptance, letting go, expressing feelings, and placing responsibility where it belongs. It is process and cannot be completed simply or quickly. However, forgiveness of yourself and of your family is a prerequisite for the next two steps.

6. Appreciating

Once you have forgiven, you can begin to appreciate what you have learned from living in your crazy family system. You can begin by appreciating the fact that you survived it all. Then you can appreciate how strong you have become. Every bad thing that happened to you has given you strength and character. Appreciate your discomfort, your pain, and your loss, for they have taught you much more than comfort and safety ever will. As much as you may hate what has happened to you, appreciate what it taught you. If your painful past has taught you nothing else, it has taught you how not to be and what not to do. Appreciate these lessons. Thank your family for getting you where you are right now. Appreciate any of the good things that they did for you. Once you have accepted the reality of your family, once you can see them with objective eyes, then you can begin to see their sacrifices, their confusions, their difficulties and struggles. You will probably recognize that these humans were trying to do what they perceived as their best effort in the situation. Appreciate that and them. Thank them, let them go, and move on.

7. Rewarding

This last step can be the best because it is often the most fulfilling to you personally. Reward yourself for surviving. Give yourself what you need. Say nice things to yourself about yourself. Begin with "I am good" and continue with "I deserve the best." Give your family members whatever credit they may deserve, but give yourself even more credit. You did it, you got here, you deserve to recognize your goodness and your effort. No one else can give you exactly what you need exactly when you need it. Give it to yourself. Do something very nice for yourself today. Give yourself something that you wish someone else would give you. Pay yourself a compliment. Do something you really want to do, just for yourself. Take care of your needs and wants. Fulfill yourself. You deserve it!

When you feel amply rewarded, you may want to share what you have learned with your family. Remember, you do not have to confront or deal with them on your issues. If you do the work on yourself, for yourself, you will have the greatest reward of all—the beginnings of maturity, mental and emotional health, belongingness, and wholeness. Share the rewards only if and when you choose to do so. Remember, you did the work and you deserve the rewards!

Let there be spaces in your togetherness.

—Kahlil Gibran

III ∞ Love and Lovers

In no arena will the reemergence of the problems that first surfaced in the family of origin be as dramatic as with the beloved other. The most pain and consequently the most growth and awareness of self occur in our love relationships. Finally we get to choose with whom we want to spend our life and time. Surely we do not expect to have the same problems that we encountered with our parents, siblings, and extended family.

Falling in Love

At some point during adolescence or early adulthood we discover the joy of being in love. At long last someone else really understands us, cares about us, and wants to be with us. *Hallelujah!* we think. *I am okay.* Someone else loves me. Our life finally seems to have meaning and purpose; we rejoice in no longer being alone. This may be the next best thing to being in the womb: We again feel safe, secure, and content. And when we become sexually involved with our beloved, we may think this is even better than being in the womb. In the beginning of the new love experience we may find it difficult to imagine that problems will occur. We feel we have transcended the mundane world; we feel euphoric. As long as this significant other person loves us, nothing else seems really important.

All of the above is why falling in love has been described as one of the altered states of consciousness, along with psychosis, being on drugs or alcohol, or being "out of it." What we are "out of" when we are experiencing an altered state is the reality of life. Altered states are transient; they cannot last forever. Even psychotics have periods of lucidity. Addicts soon learn that the high cannot be maintained for long periods. Only the love-sick ones believe that they have reached a permanent state, and they, more than any other, resent the crash back to reality when it inevitably occurs. It would seem that in the case of finding our significant other, humans have the shortest learning curve. We want so badly to feel "one" with someone else. We are so afraid of being alone and lonely. We want to be happy and we have learned that the quickest way to feel happy is to be in love.

The Dangerous Myth

So what is wrong with being in love? Why can't this be the quick fix that we all yearn for? We have grown up believing the myth that there is one right person for each of us, one soul mate to love and be loved by. We have found this person and we are happy. Why not? Why burst the illusion? If being in love makes us so happy, and if happiness in this world is so rare, why discuss this as one of our problems? The answer of course is that we must live in the reality of life in order to be real. We cannot alter ourselves indefinitely and still be. We cannot put our identity, our purpose, our very life into the hands of someone else, no matter how much we think he (or she) loves us. The main problem in our relationship with our lover is that what we have been describing above, what sounds so wonderful, is not being in love but being in need. We cannot fall in love with someone else in order to complete ourselves. If we do, we quickly find that this other person is human—flawed, imperfect, with needs and wants that do not always match our own. We can only give up so much of ourselves before we begin keeping score on what the other is giving up for us. We can only alter ourselves so much before we demand some alterations in the other. We can only ignore so much before everything that we have overlooked comes back to haunt us. All too quickly our perfect state is discovered to be imperfect and creating serious problems for us.

Facing the Reality

Let us parallel some of the problems that we encountered in infancy and childhood with what may be happening to us in our relationship with the significant other. We are still "in love," but we are beginning to come out of our altered state of consciousness in that we are starting to have problems with our beloved. We are coming back to earth and we are no longer euphoric most of the time. We are, once again, beginning to be bothered by reality. We are again feeling pain, worrying about money, taxes, and death, and the person we love is not always easy, comfortable, and loving to us. Like the infant we have exchanged safety with some attendant loneliness for comfort and nurturance with some periods of uncertainty and pain. When our beloved is loving and with us, the world feels good. But when our beloved is angry or distant or absent, our world feels terrible. We may now feel the same fear and pain of abandonment the infant felt when mother was not around. Because the fear of abandonment is overwhelming, we are prepared to do almost anything so that our significant other will not leave us and will continue to love us. We are willing to spend a lot of time and effort trying to keep this person happy. We try to change ourselves based on what he (or she) does not like about us, and we try to prevent him from becoming angry with us. Our goal is to try to keep the other happy so that we can fulfill our own needs through him. Does this sound familiar? Like the child we once were, we are again involved with issues of manipulation and control. And like the child we may begin to take on the responsibility of someone else's feelings and behavior. If we buy into the idea that we are responsible for our significant other's anger or sadness or negativity, then we are on the road toward codependency.

Responsibility Without Control

Codependency is when you care more for someone else than you do for yourself and believe that another person is more important to you than you are to yourself. It is the opposite of independence and the death of interdependence because the latter involves a mutual give-and-take process, whereas codependency means more give from one person and more take from the other. We become codependent when we take responsibility for things that are outside our control. The other person maintains control, but somehow we own the responsibility for what happens. This often results in taking the blame even though we know we are not in the wrong. Just as the young child took responsibility for the parent's behavior, now we are taking responsibility for the significant other—how he is feeling, what he is doing, and why he is not happy. It did not work in the child-parent relationship; it will not work in this one.

Reemergence of Conflict

As a child we learned that asserting identity created conflict; now we are discovering that the same thing is happening here. Our beloved may have difficulty letting us do whatever we want to do whenever we want to do it. How we spend our time and money are no longer our own decisions; our loved ones have different ideas about these issues. We may desire quiet weekends; they want activity, parties, and lots of people around. We hate sports while they cannot get enough. We love to spend money on looking good; their idea of heaven is to save, save, save, and new clothes are considered frivolous. We may think sex is great every night; they think once a week is plenty. And so it goes. What we love they do not, and yet we love them. We may even begin to discover that the very things that attracted us to them in the beginning are now beginning to repel us or, at the very least, create problems for us. What is happening?

Remember how as children we ran into problems with being good versus doing bad? How our needs for approval sometimes conflicted with what we really wanted to be doing? How our parents could be both a source of comfort and safety and also our harshest critics? Is our beloved becoming painfully like our parents? Are we beginning to experience déjà vu? How about intimacy? Can we express our feelings safely, or does our intimate other have difficulties accepting our negative feelings? We may find that it is easier to go along with what he wants than to express ourselves when it may create conflict. Can we live up to his expectations and can we live with his changing roles? If not, then we need not be surprised when we sometimes feel as helpless and hopeless as a child. We are rediscovering the very same problems that we thought this relationship would solve. What went wrong?

Familiar Patterns

The answers to the above questions are found when we contrast the patterns established in the child-parent relationship with our relationship to the loved one. While the parallels mentioned above frequently exist, there are important differences between the two. In the child-parent relationship, the parent does have the responsibility for loving and taking care of the child, who in turn has the right to be loved and cared for. The child is dependent—physically, mentally, and emotionally—on the primary caretaker for having his (or her) needs fulfilled. The parent has the power and the control over his very existence. The concept of codependence does not exist in this relationship because parents have to put the child's needs ahead of their own most of the time. This situation changes during adolescence as the teenager becomes less dependent. During this stage the parent begins the painful process of letting go, while the adolescent begins the equally painful process of assuming more control and responsibility. Perhaps one of the reasons why so many relationships with the significant other slip into the familiar patterns of the child-parent relationship is that it is so familiar. We are comfortable with what we know, even when we do not like the consequences. In the beginning of a love relationship we are usually blinded to the patterns we are establishing. We know that we need something, and our beloved seems to fill this need. We feel better when we are together, and lonely and somehow incomplete when we are apart, so we try to be with our beloved as much as possible. We pine when we are separated and spend inordinate amounts of time thinking and dreaming about him and planning for our next reunion.

During this "lovesick" process we usually forget that we do not need this other person for our survival in the way that we once needed our parents and that our partner does not owe us love or need-fulfillment in the same way that our parents owed us these things when we were little and dependent. Our lover simply does not have the responsibility for making us feel secure, happy, and complete. This is a fundamental and critical difference between this type of relationship and our parental ones. It is amazing how often this difference is overlooked, which may account for so many failed adult love relationships.

Love Versus Need

Many problems are encountered in our relationships with those we love, simply because we "love" them. They are reenacted, rediscovered, and replayed in intimate relationships because of our great need to be loved. Think how many problems are caused by this one concept: "If you love me, then . . ." The idea that our significant others owe us their love, certain ways of behaving, changes in themselves, their interest and time, and so on leads to many of the most common relationship difficulties. Possessiveness, jealousy, enmeshment, fear of separation, the inability to be oneself or express feelings, the fear of anger, physical and emotional abuse, feeling constrained or rejected—all of these have roots in the concept that our lovers are there for us and responsible for what we are feeling and that we are in turn responsible for them. Whenever we try to make our lovers a part of ourselves, so that we can be more than what we are— more alive, more complete, happier—we are functioning from *neediness*. This is not what *love* is about.

If we need others to love us in order to feel good about ourselves, then we have delegated our self-esteem to them. If we need them to behave in certain ways, or not behave in ways that we do not like, so that we can appear to look good, then we have delegated our responsibility for our own worth to them. If we need them around in order to feel loved and secure, then we have delegated our most important task, our own self-love, to them. Bless their hearts, no matter how much they love us or want to make us happy, they cannot do it. And if we begin to blame them when we do not feel loved or worthy, we compound the problems. What is jealousy if not blaming the other because we do not feel loved enough? Why would we feel possessive unless we were feeling insecure about ourselves? And what is abuse about if not the idea that someone else is to blame for our own insecurities? Maybe the simplest and most basic reason that we do not treat our most "loved" significant others in a loving manner is that we really do not love our Self, and therefore cannot really understand what the other loves about us. And when our loved ones do not behave in a loving manner to us, possibly they are really showing us how little they love their selves.

The Myth of Romance

Does all this sound as if being in love is impossible? Are you starting to feel that it is not worth the effort, and that you do not know how to have a meaningful, healthy relationship with a beloved? Do not be discouraged. Remember, we learn from our problems and mistakes. Healthy, mature relationships are worth all the time and effort we invest in them. But they do require healthy, mature selves in order to exist. We have been trained to put our self-esteem outside ourselves. We are well schooled in the art of delegation of responsibility to the ones we love. We have been blitzed by the media in the love arena. How many romantic movies exploit the premise that someone else will enhance our lives and give us purpose and meaning? How many songs do we all know with lyrics about not being able to live or be happy without our lover around?

Our concept of romantic love is based on the premise that we are incomplete if not loved by someone else, that life without a love relationship lacks meaning, and that our beloved "makes" us happy and whole. When we turn on the radio, the television, the stereo, open a magazine or romantic novel, or listen to people around us talking, we quickly discover how pervasive this myth is. If we listen to ourselves, we may hear, *So-and-so makes me feel good—makes me happy—sad—angry,* and so on. It is almost as if our feelings and behavior are hanging around outside ourselves, waiting for the "right person" to set them in motion. We have all grown up with the fantasy of "happily ever after" and have been brainwashed by fairy tales and myths of how life should be. Because of these we learn to believe that when we are not happy, whole, complete, and secure, we need to change our significant other. Our relationship must have failed because we are not living the expected ending. Therefore we must keep looking until we achieve the desired outcome, the perfect ending to our love story.

The Myth of the Hero

The only myth that fits the reality of a healthy relationship is the myth of the hero. The hero knows that life is difficult, full of pain, and unfair. He also knows that he cannot change reality.

The hero does not give up nor does he externalize these concepts; rather he looks inside and strives to do his very best, for himself. He views life as a challenge and an opportunity for growth and awareness; further he takes full responsibility for his behavior and does not assume control over others. The hero learns that the relationship with the Self is the primary relationship, and the only one he controls. He recognizes that all other relationships, especially with those he loves, are secondary to the one with the Self.

IV ∾ Problem-Solving Love and Lovers

1. Accepting

Healthy, meaningful, and life-enhancing relationships with those you love are possible. To begin with, they are about acceptance, which means that you allow others to *be,* as they are, and do not play the change game or the blame game with them. You see them as they really are, and not as you would like them to be. You accept that they cannot be perfect and there are many things that they do that do not fit into your ideas or ideals of what you want in a partner. Accept the reality that they are flawed human beings and like you possess a dark side, a shadow side, of which they may be unaware. Accept their complexities and the fact that they themselves do not always understand what they are doing or why they are doing it. You need to accept that they have insecurities and pains and fears that have nothing to do with you. Accept that you cannot know what is being thought, felt, and acted upon, unless they choose to share these things with you. Also accept that you cannot know every-thing about them, just as they cannot know all about you. But above all accept that no person was placed on this earth to take care of you or to make you happy and fulfill your needs. Accept their right to love themselves first and to do the best they can, as defined by themselves. All of this acceptance is difficult but nec-essary for a healthy relationship. It is impossible to begin to accept a significant other unless you can first accept yourself and all your own needs and rights.

2. Letting Go

Letting go means that you burst your own illusions and myths. You cannot expect perfection from your significant oth-ers simply because they love you and you love them. Let go of your concept of perfect; also let go of "shoulds." Let go of the need to control another and your need to have the other take care of you. Let go of your frustrations and negativity, as related to your partner. Let go of expectations of the other's behavior and of guilt, blame, and placing responsibility on the other for your needs.

Perhaps the most difficult thing to let go of is your fairy-tale mentality about relationships and love. You have been trained to think that when you love and are loved, your life becomes complete. You have probably learned early on that sharing ex-periences with your beloved is the happiest part of your life. You have to let go of the false concept that everything must be shared and that you can only be complete and happy when you are in a love relationship. You have to let go of needing to share, and accept the gift of sharing. In order to do this, you must let go of your need for others, and also let go of their need for you. The only way to accomplish this is to take care of your own needs first and allow others to do the same.

3. Expressing Feelings

Recognize that you will experience your entire range of emotions in all your relationships. Just because you love someone dearly does not mean that you will not feel anger, frustration, confusion, loneliness, sadness, and loss. No person can substitute for your feelings. They exist and they are not entirely dependent on the feelings or actions of your lovers, even though at times they may appear to be. You will not always respond in the same way to similar situations and you cannot always predict how you are going to feel. For example your partner says something derogatory. On one occasion you will get angry and fight back. At another time you may feel sad and retreat. And on another occasion you laugh and choose to ignore the slight. Your reaction is much more dependent on how you are feeling about yourself and the situation you are presently in than it is on the partner's behavior. And yet the attribution of your feelings is usually placed on the other. "You make me mad or sad, or whatever" delegates your feeling to your partner. And this results in a loss of control and personal power and becomes very destructive to the relationship.

It is much simpler and healthier to invest the energy into

expressing your feelings constructively rather than trying to attribute causality. When you are angry, express the anger, then let it go. You do not have to blame the other for your anger, and it may be a waste of time and energy always to investigate the reasons behind it. The mere fact that you are angry can be reason enough. Instead of placing blame for what is annoying you, simply state how you feel: not "You did that on purpose to get at me," but "I am angry and upset right now." You will stop feeling quite so angry as soon as you acknowledge and express your feeling. Treat all your feelings in the same manner: (a) acknowledge the feeling; (b) express it, at least to yourself; and (c) let it go.

Remember that one definition of intimacy is being able to express your feelings in a safe environment. You can help create such an environment by removing the blame from your significant other. Feel what you feel, express it with "I" statements, and let it go. You cannot stay angry or sad forever unless you deliberately hold on and nurture that feeling. Your beloved does not always have to be the recipient, since you can also express emotions just to yourself or to others.

4. Taking Responsibility

Just as your significant other is not responsible for your feelings, so he (or she) is also not responsible for your actions, thoughts, desires, needs, successes, and failures. In other words no one else is responsible for you. Take responsibility for your own life. After all, it is your life and no one else's. Just as you own your feelings, so also do you own your behavior. You may think that someone else is controlling you, but in reality you are choosing to allow this. When you give away your responsibility for anything you do, you give away your power and ability to be in control of yourself. This is far too much to relinquish. If a relationship is not working for you, take responsibility for your part of the dysfunction. Do something about it.

You are responsible for changing yourself and your own life. No one else is accountable for you, and you are not responsible for changing them, including your beloveds. Take responsibility for the fact that you care for your lover and that this love is a gift. Conversely recognize that you cannot control another's feelings about you, and that love is a gift to you and not your right. Take responsibility for who and what you are, and let your lovers do the same.

5. Forgiving

Begin by forgiving yourself for all the things you know you have done wrong in this and all your previous relationships. It may help to make a list of all your faults and failures and, one by one, forgive yourself for them. Forgive yourself for not being perfect. Forgive yourself for making your mistakes over and over again. Learn from these mistakes. Find the patterns that you have developed in your relationships and work on solving your own problems by fulfilling your own needs.

Then forgive your significant other and all your previous

partners for their mistakes, insecurities, and craziness. Again list the things you need to forgive, and look for patterns and similarities. These can help you learn your needs and expectations in relating to others and will teach you what you need to do for yourself. Forgive your partners for not being able to take care of you. Forgive them for being imperfect beings. Forgive them for the pain you have felt. As you forgive them, recognize that no one else, no matter how loved or loving, can do for you what you are not willing to do for yourself.

6. Appreciating

Appreciate the fact that you love. This is your greatest gift: Be thankful that you are giving it. Appreciate that by loving someone else you are enriching yourself. When you love, you expand your limits and enrich your life. Appreciate the love you feel for someone else as one of the greatest, most powerful, and most gratifying feelings you will ever know.

Then appreciate the gift that your significant other is giving you by loving you. Appreciate the fact that you are in a relationship and therefore have the possibility to experience one of life's greatest challenges. This challenge and the worth of the intimate relationship comes from the awareness that problems exist and can be worked through together. Appreciate that your growth and development as a couple depend on having problems in order to learn and refine your problem-solving skills. Appreciate that the person you love and are loved by is your greatest helpmate in facing your challenges and may be the catalyst for creating needed changes in you. Thank him for helping you grow, learn, and improve yourself.

Appreciate that all your relationships exist not always to produce comfort—you do not change in comfortable situations—but to provide challenges, help you to learn, teach you to problem-solve, and to provide encouragement. In this discouraging world your significant other may be your best ally to help you do what you must do, learn what you need to learn, and live to your fullest potential. Your beloved can be your helpmate, but he cannot live for you. Appreciate this distinction.

7. Rewarding

Reward yourself for beginning the process of having a healthy relationship. Reward yourself for all the work you have done and all the changes you have produced. Reward yourself for loving others. Give yourself a reward each time you do any of the above steps. This is difficult work and you deserve a positive reinforcement for each small step along the way. These rewards can be acknowledgments, compliments, recognition of what you have done, gifts, pats on the back, taking time for yourself, doing something that you really want to do, and being pleased with yourself.

After you have rewarded yourself, then reward your loved one. Acknowledge that you recognize and value his love for you. Express your appreciation. Give him gifts that you want to give rather than what you think he needs. Be loving, gentle, and kind. Be real. Your greatest gift to the one you love is the gift of sharing yourself as a whole, balanced, and loving partner. A healthy relationship will then become the greatest reward of all.

*All human relationships are sexual; the more intimate
they are, the more sexual they become.*

—Andrew M. Greeley

V ⌒ Sex and Sexuality

We come into this world and the first thing that defines us is
our sex. Along with this identification of male or female comes a
vast array of expectations, limitations, aspirations, and illusions. Ask expectant parents what they would wish their newborn child to be like, and after they answer "healthy," most of
these future role models will give an answer that is implicitly
based upon the sex of the child. For example a girl should be
sweet, shy, sensitive, and quiet, while a boy is expected to be
strong, brave, active, and aggressive. Many of our hopes and
dreams, as well as a large part of our training and the development of our weak egos—the esteem given to us from externals—
begin the moment we have been sexually labeled. It is no wonder, then, that so many problems center on our sex roles and
sexuality. Since much of our ego has to do with how we feel
about our bodies, our physical appearance, and consequently
how others perceive us, the relationship between our weak egos
and our sexuality is a strong one.

Sex Roles

Because sex is our first identifying characteristic and because the earliest attributions from others are based on stereotypical sex roles, it should be no surprise that many of our later problems and difficulties with relationships (with others and with our Selves) begin early in our training. We have been raised in a culture that perpetuates sexual myths, biases, and illusions. These serve to alleviate discomfort and insecurity, explain how relationships work and why they fail, provide communication topics, be entertaining (everyone relates to gender jokes), and provide a sense of belonging because we experience the same types of problems. All of us probably feel very comfortable when discussing the opposite sex (especially what is wrong with them) with members of our own sex. This tendency is reflected by the current trend to explain relationships and teach communication skills by focusing on the differences between the sexes. We can be comforted by the concept that both sexes communicate differently, perhaps even for different purposes, until we are personally involved in painful miscommunications with those we love.

Blaming our lack of communication or understanding on gender differences may actually, in the long run, lead to alienation from one half the world's population. This is especially true when these sexual variances are implicitly attributed to heredity, meaning that they are innate or wired in, and therefore unchangeable. Generalities, such as "Men are stronger and less emotional than women" or "Women are more nurturing than men" can be dangerous because they perpetuate the myth that men and women belong to different species and because they focus on differences rather than similarities. This is not to say there are no differences between the sexes (of course there are!), but it is not the obvious differences that create most difficulties. It is the attribution of genetic characteristics—therefore unchangeable—to what is actually learned differences—therefore changeable—that most often divides the sexes. When this occurs, more problems are created than are solved or resolved. The understanding that external styles may be different but internal feelings and motivations are the same will alleviate many of these problems.

Sex Differences

The reality, as demonstrated by extensive research, is that there are very few innate (genetic) differences between the sexes at birth. It was only discovered in the last few decades that all human embryos spend the first weeks of their lives as females, and that in order for males to develop, there must be the addition of the male hormone androgen. This hormone changes the sexual organs into male, but the effects on other vital organs—the heart, kidneys, lungs—are unknown. And what about the brain? If indeed males are inherently distinct from females in the ways they think, feel, process, communicate, act and react, desire and dream, then that which has occurred in the womb must cause these differences. This hormonal addition, which alters the sexual organs, would also have to significantly alter the structure of the brain and its subsequent development in order for emotional and cognitive differences between the sexes to be innate rather than learned. There simply is no clear evidence that this is the case.

Years of research focused on sexual differences has not demonstrated or substantiated such differences due solely to sex. Until very recently extensive research had only demonstrated four clear inherent differences between males and females. These four differences are relatively minor ones and in no way account for the common idea that men and women are two different species of human.

Genetic Differences

The four innate sexual differences validated by research are:

1. Males are better with visual-spatial tasks, such as rotating a three-dimensional object in their heads. More simply, men can more easily read a map without rotating it.
2. Females speak earlier and develop better language skills until they reach puberty, when the differences equalize. The concept of female intuition seems to be validated by this earlier interactional emphasis. Women also tend to do better than men with verbal memory skills and abstract mental tasks.
3. Males tend to favor their right ears while listening; females show no preference and use both ears equally.
4. Males have more severe responses to physiological stress,

which may account for their having more and earlier heart attacks than women.

There is some very recent research indicating that the way that males and females deal with emotions may be a result of differences in brain functioning. This could help explain why males react more physically to emotions while women tend to react with words, facial expressions, and gestures. If these findings are consistently validated, they will be the first studies indicating that some emotional responses are genetically wired in, rather than learned behavior. More importantly for this discussion they would indeed indicate that emotional reactions are innately different in the male and female sexes.

Even with all the research done to date, it seems difficult to justify the popular idea that we are two entirely different species, from different planets, who are wired so differently that we must learn how the other sex thinks, feels, and behaves in order to communicate with and understand each other. The different ways in which men and women express some feelings may be genetically determined; the fact that we all feel the same feelings may be the more critical issue. Focusing on the differences between the sexes may be great material for comedy acts, television sitcoms, movies, and popular workshops, but any theory that is based on finding differences rather than searching for similarities will eventually lead to severe misunderstandings, dangerous attributions, and perhaps even alienation.

Disproving the Myth

The reality about the male-female dilemma is that once we move past the physical, we are much more similar than we are different. And even at the physical level there exists the popular myth that males are always stronger than females. Research and mortality statistics indicate that females are physiologically stronger from birth until puberty. With regard to mental and emotional characteristics, not one of the four proven innate sexual differences has to do with feelings, thought processes, needs, desires, or basic insecurities. And the most recent research only deals with a genetic basis for some difference in the expression of feelings and not the possession of these feelings. Culturally we like to think that women are emotionally stronger than men, whom we consider better at objective, dispassionate thinking. The Western model reinforces these sexual differences partly because our male-dominated culture values rationality over emotionality. Women are reinforced for relating and exhibiting "people skills," while men are encouraged to be stronger, more objective, and stoic. Society teaches and rewards these distinctions because the skills required of leaders and heads of organizations are thought to be the ones that men "naturally" possess. This myth is slowly being disproved, but the subsequent stereotypes have been ingrained in our thinking.

Thus the obvious may be difficult to accept: Men and women belong to the same species and are therefore very much alike across all dimensions. As we slowly reject the stereotype of the unfeeling male, we discover that men are as emotional as women. We have been trained to think that women feel more, but a body of research indicates that men feel equally or sometimes even more deeply, depending on the issue. For example studies have shown that college-aged males fall more deeply in love than their female peers. Both sexes are also very much alike mentally. This fact is slowly being substantiated as more women are allowed into every facet of modern society, where they are succeeding. The myth that men and women are significantly different has been and will continue to be very destructive as long as the expectations about what each can be, do, think, feel, and want are limited by sex roles. Furthermore this limitation is destructive to the concept and practice of the human spirit. Above all, we could not relate to the other, our so-called opposite, if there were not similarities between us. It is the sameness between us that we understand and relate with; this sameness derives from each of us having a masculine and feminine side within us.

The Myth and the Model

If many of our sexual myths have been disproved by research, why, then, are they still so prevalent in our thinking and behavior? They are derived directly from our training; they form the foundation of the Western model. This is a linear, work-related model (you are what you do) that emphasizes external goals and definitions of success. In terms of sexuality this Western model is clearly patriarchal, an overtly masculine framework for a culture historically dominated by men. This model stems from male-dominant philosophies, values, and especially a masculine religion. (The concept of God from the time of Judaism has been of a male deity. Before that, God was perceived as either female or androgynous.) This masculine Doing model has persisted as the framework for how we should live our lives because something in it works. Our Puritan ethics respond positively to a model that emphasizes work and a linear learning process. Perhaps society has adopted and reinforced it because it is familiar and therefore does not threaten the male perspective.

The Facade

Interestingly women's liberation movements, which set out purposefully to change and expand the male perspective, ended up joining it. Women reacted against men by behaviorally copying men. All too often they imitated the worst masculine traits and mimicked the most aggressive and adversarial male behavior, thus demonstrating that much of so-called male behavior is learned rather than innate. In actuality they reinforced the masculine perspective instead of expanding it to include the feminine view. Most of our female role models—especially those portrayed on television and in film—have relinquished the best female traits and behavior, those attributes that make being feminine a virtue. Instead they have adopted the external traits that superficially define male strength. They have taken on the facade of masculinity and left behind their own femininity and integrity.

We may indeed laugh at Roseanne and Murphy, or admire

Thelma and Louise, but do we really want to be like them if we are women? Can we relate to them if we are men? Do they represent the best of anything? Do we like them? Do we want to act as they do? Hopefully not, because these characters are not balanced, whole, or real. In their efforts to change the biases, break the stereotypes, and expand their roles and identities, they are creating a new facade, a new caricature—the pseudomale female. By denying the true reality of themselves, they have lost their validity. True masculinity and true femininity have integrity, great value, and innate worth, and are remarkably similar. In recognizing our humanness we become aware of our duality; we have both masculine and feminine sides. When we deny one of these, to ourselves and to society, we become unidimensional and merely a facade.

The Power Quest

The rebellion against men that has occurred over the last few decades is in part based on several myths perpetuated by the Western model that life is Doing, and doing means work. Because the model stresses work, it is not a coincidence that men have had all or most of the power in the workplace. Our cultural consensus is that men have power and that women want more of it. Because we are taught to confuse life with work, it is natural to believe that power at work is life power. And because more men are dominant at work than women, it is natural to assume that this dominance defines who is powerful. Therefore it is not uncommon to see women become aggressive in order to feel powerful, to give up empathy and nurturance in order to be perceived as strong and objective, and to stop feeling and relating in order to sharpen their objective rational thinking. Are these not the very qualities against which women rebelled: male aggressiveness; greed; lack of caring; insensitivity; insecurity reflected by high needs for power and control; cold, objective rationality, and calculated cruelty?

Meanwhile what has happened to some of the men? When women started their search for power and tried dramatically to change the male-dominated model by bashing men while at the same time imitating them, many men simply became confused. They did not know what to do, how to think or behave, whether or not to take the blame. What used to be courtesy now became discrimination; what used to be a compliment or a prelude to a relationship now became harassment. Anything "masculine" was suddenly controversial at best and at worst despicable. The good guys no longer knew how to be good, and the bad guys as usual did not care. As is so often the case, confusion opened the door to paradoxical change. In their own confusion and frustration many men discovered their true natures and got in touch with their feminine sides. Their lack of certainty regarding behavior and emotions allowed them to expand their repertoires and become more feeling. Those men who tried to give up some of their power to the women demanding it discovered that they had much more internal and interpersonal strength. They learned what women were quickly forgetting—that the feminine side is covertly powerful.

Quiet power has always been stronger than overt power. The only strength that is worthwhile is internal, that which we feel toward ourselves. And this cannot be bought or given, forced, coerced, or demanded from others. Internal power (self-worth) is born in confusion and uncertainty and a certain amount of humility. Women have developed it through centuries of frustration, oppression, and the need to problem-solve in order to exist and ensure the survival of their offspring. They found internal strength out of desperation and confusion and lost that strength in the quest for external power. And as women were forgetting the value of quiet power, men were learning about it in their struggle to appease the angry women. Ironically these men became balanced and whole, while many newly powerful women wondered why they had lost their sense of balance. Perhaps the secret is simple: We need to be multidimensional; we need to accept our dualistic natures.

Finding the Balance

Our humanness consists of covert feminine power combined with overt masculine strengths and actions. It is composed of both a passive being side and an active doing side. When we recognize the value of both within our Selves, we become complete and secure. Whether we are physically male or female, combining our dual natures and forgoing sexual facades and societal sex roles allows us to become whole human beings. Then we have integrity. Then we are one with our true Self, our nature, our destiny, and our spirituality.

Unfortunately there is little training available to teach us how to be whole rather than unidimensional. Can we even begin to imagine having a baby and not being concerned about its sex? Can we envision living in a society that assumes we are both masculine and feminine, and that, beyond procreation, the physical body is not one of our most important characteristics? In such an ideal, dual-focused culture there would be no competition between the sexes because it would be assumed that everyone had similar attributes. A power struggle between men and women would be meaningless. Discussions regarding behavior and communications would focus on similarities rather than differences. Being male or female would simply be perceived as nature's way of making sure the species survived. Beyond that the real meaning—the true importance of our lives—would have nothing to do with our sex. Can we imagine no distinction between our sex roles—that mother and father perform in the same way, that sister and brother are truly equal, that husband and wife become meaningless labels? If we can imagine giving up our sex roles and stereotyped identities, can we then see how our problems with sexuality would drastically change?

Developing Duality

Of course life without sexual stereotypes will not happen in the foreseeable future, and maybe this is a good thing because there is much to be learned about our masculine and feminine roles. The opposite sex can teach us about the side of our Self that has not been acknowledged or reinforced, our "hidden side." We can learn a great deal about our own fears and inhibitions by focusing on what others do differently. By being open and interested in what is strange, foreign, or frightening to us, we can become more accepting and aware of what is hidden inside ourselves.

If we are afraid of the opposite sex, we need to become familiar with it in order to overcome this fear. If we are fascinated by the other sex, we need to observe it more closely and discover similarities; our fascination will change into a realistic recognition that we are all very much alike. If we despise or denigrate the opposite sex, we need to recognize that we are hating that side of ourselves. And if we are more comfortable with the opposite sex than with our own, we need to acknowledge that aspect of our inner selves that needs to be developed. When we become comfortable with the unfamiliar side of ourselves, we become friends with our whole selves. We can strive toward the balance and learn to be complete humans by appreciating both sides of our Self. Sex roles, by definition, limit us to the external self and ignore the totality and duality of the whole. When we move beyond them, we become truly sexual.

In order to do so, we have to learn to focus on process and similarities rather than on content and differences. For example men and women share fear of the other's power. Men express fear of being emotionally hurt, sexually manipulated, or vulnerable and therefore victimized. Women are afraid of being physically hurt, sexually harassed and abused, or of dealing with their victimization for fear of retaliation. The reasons for these fears are different, yet both share the feeling of fear and the sense of loss of control. When relationship discussions focus on content (the reasons for the fear), neither sex will relate to the other. However, when these discussions move into process (the sharing of the feelings of fear and loss of control), meaningful communication and intimacy result.

Sex Versus Sexuality

Sex roles are about limits; the act of sex can be about expansion. Perhaps the single most liberating behavior that we are capable of is the act of sexual intercourse. Andrew Greeley, a Catholic priest and author, discusses the act of sex as a rehearsal for our ultimate unification with God. It is the closest thing on earth to feeling joined, experiencing universal belongingness, becoming one with the whole, being absorbed into the Higher Power, being in the light, dissolving, losing oneself, and paradoxically discovering that we are more than we ever knew. Having sex can be the most beautiful, life-enhancing activity we experience, full of meaning and wonder. It can also be one of the worst possible activities, full of darkness and rage. Sex, like most of our gifts from God, has the power to be both incredible and terrible at the same time. It is not accidental that we have such complex and mixed feelings about the sex act and that it creates many problems for us at all stages of our lives. It is no wonder that we are confused about the difference between sex and sexuality.

With very few exceptions, most of our problems with sexuality have nothing to do with our physiological bodies. The vast majority occur from our mental and emotional states. Sexuality is not really about sex—the sexual act—but is much more connected to our body image, weak ego, and the degree of self-esteem that we possess. Sexuality is a natural aspect of most living things and, when left alone, is pure joy to feel and see. However, among humans, it is never left alone. Some of our earliest problems occur when the natural sexuality of the child causes discomfort to the parents and they send out messages (often nonverbal) that this behavior is "bad, dirty, to be avoided, not acceptable, uncomfortable," or else they ignore it and the child notices the lack of attention. Often our earliest perception regarding our sexuality is that it produces discomfort or anxiety in those we love and want attention from. If we are compliant, we will try to change or stop doing things that bother our parents. If we are rebellious, we may increase these acts in order to upset (and thereby gain attention from) these adults. We have learned as children that our sexuality has a clear effect upon others. We have already begun to be dependent upon their perceptions about us. Thus our sexual problems have begun.

These difficulties multiply geometrically when we engage in sexual intercourse. Society, usually through covert education, teaches us that sex and sexuality are the same thing. Sexuality is confused with the activity of having sex. We learn, while we are very young, that sex is complicated, difficult, emotional, and produces major problems but that it is also something everyone wants to have. We also discover that people have sex for many reasons: to gain control, satisfy physical desires, fill other needs such as security or popularity, enhance worth, feel loved, feel needed, make money, rebel, be "sexy," or to belong. And we quickly learn that there is a dark side to sex and that abuse, harassment, prostitution, sex with children, sex with animals, and other strange or perverted sexual acts exist. We are simultaneously taught that sex is desirable and to be avoided, is very good and also quite evil, people love and hate it, and that it is simply a physical act and yet involves many complicated aspects. Most of us develop our fascination and repulsion for sex at an early age, and we continue this dichotomous reaction to it throughout our lives.

The Simplicity of Sex

The only pure reasons for the sexual act are procreation and unification with the beloved. These are simple reasons and require the existence of reciprocal feelings and mutual desires between both partners. If sex is used for any other purpose, problems will occur. If used for ulterior motives or as a goal in and of itself—just to do it—it will lack meaning. The act of intercourse seems to have been designed not just for procreation (or we would have very few sexual experiences), but for life enhancement and self-expansion as well. Sex will not lead to love, nor will it lead to awareness, emotional connection, or true intimacy with the partner unless the potential for these already exist before the act is consummated. (This is not what the romantic myth teaches us, nor what movies portray.) Difficulties occur when we attribute any other goal to the sexual act. Our culture, defined by the goal-oriented Doing model, trains us to believe just the opposite: Sex is bonding (unwanted sex is one of the least bonding acts imaginable); sex will lead to love (it does not create love but can enhance or encourage the preexisting potential for it); sex can be used to gain power and control (this common misuse rapidly boomerangs and comes around in a multitude of societal problems); and sex is dirty, confusing, and demeaning and therefore must be controlled (it is a natural process and works amazingly well when treated as such).

Society, in the form of organized religions, institutions, and public education, has done a terribly destructive thing to *sex*. It is rare to find a sexually liberated American, even though we tend to think of ourselves as a sexually liberated country. We may well be the culture most obsessed with the idea of sex, but we are also one of the most confused about the place for it in our society. We have been in political, moral, and legal controversies concerning it for the past four decades at least. Issues concerning abortion, homosexuality, and sex education have become controversial political, legal, and media topics. And we seem no closer to being comfortable with it, in spite of all the attention. One thing has become painfully clear: We cannot seem to find a common ground from which to legislate, educate, organize, and deal with sex and related issues (sexual preference, sexual diseases, appropriate sexual behaviors, pornography, incest, abuse, harassment, abortion, promiscuity, prostitution, disease, and entertainment, among others). The answer to all this may be quite simple. Perhaps we need to conceive of sex as a more natural and uncomplicated process, with simpler rules and clearer, stronger punishments for violating them. Maybe it is too late for such simplicity in society, but it is not too late for individuals to learn how to think, feel, and behave about it for their own sexual selves.

The Obsession

Most of us have learned to feel guilt or anxiety regarding our own sexuality, which usually manifests in how we feel about our physical self. There is usually some part of our external body that causes us discomfort or embarrassment. Many of us never get past the problems caused by having a poor body image. This internal image is often more powerful than the actual reality. Our Western model (covert cultural training) has combined with the media (overt cultural brainwashing) to create a nation obsessed with being slim and young. Almost all facets of society, including medical and educational institutions, seem to have joined in this current obsession. Far too many of us are overly concerned with our physical bodies and hypercritical of our looks, to the point of becoming pathological. Eating disorders among our young are now epidemic; at least half of the females in their late teens and twenties have some degree of difficulty with bulimia, anorexia, or overeating. This preoccupation with external appearance has become destructive to the emotional, physical, and mental health of the country. And it seems that our best and brightest, our role models, are the most susceptible. Our own eyes can show us what the statistics confirm: We are a nation of disproportionately overweight individuals, and very few of us will ever look like the supposed ideal that is being constantly thrown at us.

But at the same time we are not being allowed to be comfortable in our own bodies unless they match this crazy, unrealistic standard. This ideal standard is so limited and difficult to obtain that we pay those incredibly few who meet it exorbitant sums of money and excessive adulation, just because their bodies match this ideal. Their talent, skills, character, intelligence, education, personality, or humanity seem to be of no importance. Their physical appearance is the only important criterion for instant fame and fortune; their perfect bodies and faces are all that matter. As a result the ideals of being whole and balanced and the search for true meaning in life, which could be taught by society and its institutions, are lost in the quest for the perfect body. This leads to emphasis on superficiality and mediocrity. Unfortunately our culture rewards that which is profitable and promotes that which is popular. At this time our conception of beauty is the perfect, slim, young body, which very few of us have. It is no wonder that so many of us feel lost and that we are not "good" enough. Our personal search for worth and meaning will take us off the popular model and away from society's rewards and may leave us feeling quite alone and confused. We may hate the superficial values being promulgated, but at the same time how many of us like or love the way we look? How many of us are truly at home and comfortable in our own skins? How many of us have really moved past the sexual brainwashing?

The Reality of Sexuality

Following all this, it becomes relatively simple to understand why in this culture there is so much insecurity related to sexuality. We have been taught that our sexuality is determined by the notice and appreciation of others, usually of the opposite sex. If these others think we are sexual, then we think we are. If they do not, then we cannot be. This is brainwashing at its finest, and also destructive and pervasive nonsense. The truth is that we are all sexual beings. We are sexual, whether we engage in sexual activities or not. We are sexual, no matter what anyone else thinks or even what we think. Our sexuality is as much a part of our being alive as are our beating hearts. We are sexual because we cannot not be. And our sexuality, or the manner in which we demonstrate its nature, is manifested by our feelings and perceptions about ourselves. As a matter of fact it is not totally in our control, as it is innate and part of our very being.

Because of this it is possible for others to perceive our sexual nature, our inherent sexuality, without us recognizing or being aware of it. Sexuality is like our skin—parts of it are always being shown and it is impossible to cover all of it up. The important realization here is that what we think and feel about it to ourselves are the only things that really matter. What others think and feel are not as important, even though we may badly want them to be. Paradoxically those lucky or very wise ones who recognize within themselves that they are sexual are perceived to be so by others, no matter what so-called contradictory evidence may exist. They may not fit society's definition of attractive, they may even be obese or very plain, but when they are in touch with their inner beauty, their true sexuality, it shines out for others to see. Conversely the most attractive people who do not believe in their own sexuality, but need constant external confirmation, are usually perceived as insecure and rather pathetic.

Our culture teaches us that our physical attributes define us. If we believe and try to live according to this premise, society punishes us by withholding the approval, acceptance, and appreciation that we desperately crave. The best way to resolve this dilemma is not to concentrate on the physical at all, but to work on developing and increasing self-esteem. When we learn to love ourselves, we will naturally love our sexual natures and be comfortable with our sexuality. If we do not love ourselves, our perceived sexuality is just part of the facade that we present to others.

What to Do

As mentioned, sex and sexuality cannot be used to obtain power and control without creating unnecessary problems. The best way to prevent this is to do exactly what we need to do to get in touch with our own sexuality. We can focus on how we feel about ourselves and not on how others feel about us. We can change our needs for power over others into feeling powerful about ourselves. Also we can learn that we cannot control others in any way unless they allow us to have the illusion of control. If we use our sexuality to gain power, to manipulate others, or as a means to something else, invariably it will backfire and we will lose. This cannot work, we cannot win, because sexuality is not a commodity or an external attribute to be bartered or used; it is simply inseparable from our own natures. If we concentrate on developing character, integrity, and balance and worry less about being sexual, we will have it all. The same is true for experiencing healthy sex.

As many have painfully learned from experience, sex for the wrong reasons can cause loneliness, separation from others, alienation from the world, and sadness. Sex without intimacy may actually increase our worst fears of abandonment and loneliness and lead to destructive, unhealthy relationships. The paradox here is that we often create the very things we are trying to escape from when we engage in frivolous or meaningless sex. The possibilities for having low self-esteem and feelings of being empty, used, sad, and lonely are increased. Indiscriminate sex may lead to intense unhappiness, anger, frustration, confusion, and feelings of betrayal. As painful as these experiences are, they are valuable if they teach us to determine when we can and when we cannot have sexual interactions. We may discover that we need some rules to help us make this determination and that we feel more comfortable and fulfilled when we follow them. What we learn about both sex and our own sexuality, similar to everything else in life, is process. We are continually in a stage of discovery. Thus all experience, particularly the painful, functions to teach us something of value.

Abusing Sex

Sexual abuse has occurred in all cultures, although it has historically been repressed or denied. Recently it has become a major concern for this society, probably due to the fact that victims have finally been given permission to speak out. This abuse is rarely about sex itself or an expression of sexuality, but rather it is about the abuser using sex as a weapon or a means to some other end. The problems that are created are never the fault of the victims, even though many victims assume some responsibility for them. In truth they have no more responsibility for this abuse than they would if they were involved in an automobile accident in which the other driver crossed the median and hit them. In this case no one blames the victim for being hit; he just happened to be in the wrong spot at the wrong moment. So it is exactly with sexual abuse. These victims would heal much faster, with lessened stigma and no need for shame, if all of us understood that the victim is always an innocent party. Perhaps we, as a society, need to adopt the following simple rule: Sexual intercourse is only for consenting, equally vulnerable, and equally mature partners. If there were no extenuating circumstances and no exceptions to this rule, how simple it would be, then, to make the sexual act a criminal one when one of the participants is a victim of the other. The immature or unconsenting partner would always be a victim. This is one of those rare cases in which the attribution of blame would be simple and the awareness of the true nature and purpose of the sexual act would be critical.

Sexual abuse is a problem caused by anger, frustration, unrealized needs for power, and pathological needs for control. It is the result of forcing insecurities and needs onto another and is rarely a crime of sexual passion. Usually it is a passionately violent offense against sexuality and the true nature of sex. The abusers are actually turning against their own sexuality when they use sex to exploit and hurt others. Sexual abuse, then, becomes the exact opposite of the highest potential for sex, which is the joining together as rehearsal for true unification. Abused sex is the ultimate act of alienation because it involves using our most intimate expression of love as a tool for hatred, power, and oppression. The responsibility is always on the abuser. The sexual act, similar to any other choice of behavior under our control, can be used for evil and will result in dual alienation, from the true Self and from God. This may well be an apt description of being in hell.

Taking the Risk

The sharing of loving sex with another may well be our closest earthly connection to heaven. In order to have this joyous experience, we need to be willing to risk ourselves to the unknown. Great sex results from letting go; the first thing to abandon is the need for control. Then we must relinquish our fears and anxieties and rise above our insecurities. Most of our common sexual dysfunctions stem from these problems and our inability to take a risk. Healthy sex requires the feeling of worthiness—we need to know that we deserve this gift—combined with the awareness of our own vulnerability. In the presence of such a gift we become humble.

Great sex is great paradox. In the beginning there is much focus on the partner—how he is feeling, what is occurring with him. Then, as the pleasure progresses, the focus shifts to the self—how wonderful it feels—and all we can think of is what is happening to us. Finally all awareness of self and other disappears; the climax results from the complete letting go of all control. This is the moment of unification; it can only happen after the separation—the unawareness of all, the detachment from all—occurs. Perhaps in this sense the sexual act is a metaphor for life development. We begin with great attachment to the other and focus on him to fulfill our needs. We learn to detach from others and focus on fulfilling our own needs and desires. We then develop a heightened awareness of love, for the self and for the other. Finally we let go of everything—all fears, all need for control, and all attachments. As soon as we risk and relinquish, we experience the paradox of unification: When we let go, we become part of the Whole.

The Gift of Sex

Whether or not we believe in the paradox of unification, there is one fact that needs to be mentioned because it is something that we are rarely taught and that only very few enlightened souls seem to discover. Sex is *fun!* (It has even been called God's joke.) Sex, when preceded by love, respect, appreciation, and humility, is great fun. Our enjoyment of sex is a gift; we are blessed with the ability to have sexual intercourse for the pure pleasure of it. As is true of all gifts from God, the choices for using or misusing, comprehending or misunderstanding the beauty and relevance of what is being given create incredible dilemmas. Therefore the act of sex as an expression of love, as play, as great fun, and as the potential for true belonging is not comparable with the act of sex as a mechanism for violence, an expression of contempt, and the potential for alienation from others and from the soul. All gifts from God seem to have both light and dark sides; all contain choices for positive use or misuse. Thus in order to comprehend our sexual natures and minimize the risk of abusing the gift, it is necessary for us to learn how to resolve our difficulties with sex and sexuality. These problems, with few physical exceptions, can be attributed to our lack of self-esteem. They are manifested when we are unable to love ourselves. Trying to solve them by changing our physical bodies is comparable to trying to return to the womb. Both are impossible; both waste our valuable time. Yearning for the unattainable prevents us from doing the work we need to do in order to recognize the innate beauty of our sexuality and the gift of sex.

Sexual Partners

The gender of the sexual partner, as long as both are consenting adults, is a personal decision and is best controlled by the participating individuals. Sexual preference is not always about choice or training; a genetic predisposition to either the opposite or the same sex is strongly indicated. Many of us were born "lucky" in that we desire and are attracted to the opposite sex. We are lucky because heterosexual preferences minimize confusion and controversy and are strongly reinforced by society and family. Some of us were born not feeling comfortable with the gender indicated by the physical exterior. Some men have described the phenomenon and pain of being a "woman trapped in a man's body." And some women feel that they are males in a female form. Some of these people are also attracted to the opposite sex, the gender opposite from their internal sexual nature, rather than their external manifestation. There are also those who are comfortable with their gender and attracted to the same gender. The homosexual attraction may or may not be in their conscious choice. All of these possibilities, and others, exist and are the reality of human sexuality.

When healthy sex is defined as the loving act between mutually consenting adults, then homosexual sex will not be considered unhealthy. When deviant sex is defined as that which victimizes or abuses one of the partners, or that which exploits the vulnerable or nonconsenting partner, then same-gender sex will no longer be considered deviant. For both definitions the gender of the partners is not the important consideration. Unfortunately this society currently seems more concerned with gender issues than with abuse and victimization ones. Thus it labels everything except traditional (heterosexual) sex as deviant, but does not always label sexual abuse as such. It is insane that healthy, loving sex between gay men or lesbians is treated as abnormal and as being against God and society, while unhealthy, victimizing heterosexual activities are often ignored or downplayed by society and Church. If our society removed the stigma from the adult homosexual by adopting the above definitions, many problems would be resolved. To begin with, an individual's sexual partner and his (or her) own manifestation of sexuality would become a personal decision rather than a societal problem. Society cannot control either our sexuality or the kind of person to whom we are attracted; whenever it attempts to legislate the impossible, unnecessary problems are created. Whenever we define another's deviance by our prejudices, we ignore the real problems and focus on the wrong resolutions.

Sexual Acceptance

The critical issue regarding sexual partners and preferences is for each of us to be true to the Self. Whom we choose to have sex with is our business, as long as we are not causing pain or creating a victim. Sexual acceptance is really as simple as the idea that if we are not personally interested in sex with another person, then who he or she is interested in is none of our concern. This is an adult choice and assumes the participants are both adults. Insecurities seem to run rampant when we become preoccupied with the sex lives of others. In this arena society itself is incredibly insecure. However, cultural insecurity does not have to be our problem or a reflection of our own insecurities. Being means accepting; we are who we are, and others are also who they are. This acceptance is total—there is no exemption because someone is sexually different from us. If we are comfortable in our own skins and enjoy healthy sex, we can allow others the same rights. If we are not comfortable with ourselves, it will be difficult to allow others to be. We will project our insecurities on to them and try to change their behavior. This is futile, as we can only change our own Selves. Our sex roles have been culturally determined; our sexual identity and sexuality are part of our unique personal humanness.

VI ⌐ Problem-Solving Sex and Sexuality

1. Accepting

The acceptance of another's sexuality and preferences is impossible unless you are able to accept your own sexuality, sexual desires, and choices, without fears, shame, or guilt. The first step in this process is to move beyond the boundaries of your sex role. Because this is such an important characteristic of the Western model (a male-oriented one), you have been trained since birth to think in terms of limitations and differences between the sexes. While differential thinking may initially create a feeling of power or superiority and may function to alleviate anxiety, it will eventually lead to alienation and even more personal insecurity. Practice accepting the concept that you are related and similar to everyone; you share human traits and characteristics. Instead of focusing on the differences, look for the similarities.

Accept the fact that, except for relatively few external features (sexual organs, body size, weight) and surprisingly few internal characteristics, you are much more like the opposite sex than you are different. Move past the societal stereotypes and accept that thinking, feeling, creating, acting and reacting, talking, listening, relating, and loving are human traits that you share with all. When you find yourself reverting to the habit of thinking in terms of us or them, accept that this is just your training and move past what you have learned. When you can really accept our shared humanness, you will be able to stop thinking and acting according to your learned sex role.

Moving past the limitations of stereotypical thinking is much easier than accepting your own sexuality. It is always easier to do something that involves others than it is to focus entirely on the Self. Again this is because of faulty training. Knowing who you really are, what you really want and like, what pleases you, can be painful and even traumatic if you are repressing this awareness due to guilt, fear, or anxiety. Because of your culturally trained attitudes about sex, you have surely experienced sexual guilt or fear at some point in your life. The way that you learned about sex as a child, unless your earliest instruction was given by sexually healthy adults, will have produced guilt that you have done something wrong or fear that you are in some way abnormal. Sexual myths are much more frightening and have a much longer impact on your life than does your developmentally appropriate fear of monsters and the dark.

Accept that sex is a natural process and that much of what you have learned about it is as mythical as the monster under your bed. Society has made sex the monster inside your bed. Accept that, once again, society is wrong. Then accept that you cannot change society, but you can right this wrong for yourself, and perhaps even become a role model of healthy sexuality for others. Healthy sex occurs when you recognize that it is a gift from God to be enjoyed by consenting adults who wish to express their love and caring. Healthy sexuality, on the other hand, has nothing to do with the sexual act. Instead, it is the reflection of comfort in your own skin, the awareness of your Self in this world, and the genuine loving of all parts of yourself. When you have self-esteem, your love of Self, you manifest your own sexuality. The two are inseparable.

2. Letting Go

Let go of the idea that sex is wrong or bad or dirty. Let go of your fears that you are wrong or bad or dirty. And above all let go of any ideas that you can use sex for other purposes—power, control, emotional fulfillment, to create esteem, to create love, to create belongingness—and have healthy sexual relationships. Recognize that there are two equally valid reasons for the sexual act: to create babies and to enhance the intimacy in your relationship. Yes, sex may be bonding for you, but only if you already have the potential for that bonding. The act of sex may be your most loving manifestation of feelings you already have. It is fulfillment of your physical needs, but it is also an awareness of your emotional desires. Sex can relieve your stress and tension; it will also produce stress when you use it for the wrong reasons.

Above all, let go of the idea that your sexuality is dependent upon your physical body or upon any external factor. Someone else's opinion of your sexiness does not make you sexual. Anyone else's evaluation is simply a projection of their own definition of sexual. Let go of the popular concept that your worth or ability to be loved is dependent upon looking sexy or physically attractive. Try to let go of the massive brainwashing that you have been exposed to from the media. Get rid of your cultural conditioning of paying attention only to the externals. Unlike true beauty, which exists inside, physical beauty is determined by the time you live in. Therefore it is transient and constantly changes. What was beautiful in earlier times is not considered beauty now, and what is now will not be in the next century. Let go of the time and energy spent trying to conform to the present concept of beauty.

Know that there is true beauty inside of you right now and that this will be exposed as soon as you realize your internal worth and goodness and discover your relationship with God. When you concentrate only on the externals, you become a beautiful facade that is only surface deep. This superficial beauty quickly becomes boring and meaningless to others and, most especially, to your Self. Let go of this self-destructive fixation on your external appearance; know that it is another addiction of this culture. Reverse the amount of time, energy, and effort you currently spend on the external versus the internal self. Exercise, eat what is important, and worry about your physical body to the extent that you are healthy. The rest of your concern needs to be focused on discovering your internal self and the beauty that lies within you.

3. Expressing Feelings

Perhaps there is no other area of your life that has created such contradictions and confusions as the one consisting of your feelings of love and your sexual behavior. Most likely you were brought up to believe that love and sex are part of the same process, or are synonymous. In these more liberal times it is usually assumed that once you recognize your feeling of love for another, the next step is to go to bed together. Or, in the opposite case, when you are sexually active, then you will fall in love. This latter progression has been attributed more to women than to men, demonstrating sex-role biases as well as creating confusion between sex and love. And when you reflect upon what you have been trained to feel about your sex role, being female or being male, then the possibility for even more confusion exists. You have to be very healthy and balanced to get past all the insane and destructive but powerfully addictive training you have encountered along the way.

If you are not sure what you feel about any of this, do not panic. Being confused is normal, natural, and not a bad place to begin. Do not try to sort out your feelings too quickly, or you will arrive at superficial solutions. The most important thing to recognize is that you have already begun the process of getting in touch with your Self and that you have your entire lifetime to learn and grow. Being comfortable and knowing all the answers are not the purpose of your life.

Perhaps you can begin by thinking about how you feel about your sex role. Do you like being male or female? Do you like members of your own sex? How about the opposite sex? What do you feel about them? What attributes about them do you most like? Most dislike? Wish you had? Try to get in touch with your feelings about having both masculine and feminine sides within yourself. Does this scare you? Feel uncomfortable? Embarrass you? Do not filter your feelings, because you will only be repressing important awareness from yourself. If they overwhelm or scare you, get help and support. Remember, the feelings will pass; you cannot control them. You do not have to act on any of them. You do not have to be afraid of the opposite-sexed side within you, or act on it, or let it embarrass or control you. You do need to become aware of it and to be aware of your emotions and why you are feeling what you are. Most of the time your feelings will reflect your reaction to or confirmation of your training. They will also indicate your skepticism about it. But above all they will point out your insecurities and give you a precise map of what you need to work on within yourself, in order to be balanced, healthy, and whole.

Your feelings about the sex act also reflect your training, unfulfilled needs, and insecurities. Your fears, anger, biases, phobias, sadness, frustrations, and confusion all teach you more about your culture, your faulty training, the model, and your value system than they probably teach you about sex itself. The sexual act is a natural one, which has become perverted by erroneous information and the imposition of values, expectations, and labels. These indicate more about society than about the sexual act. As long as you are not personally creating harm or pain to anyone else, what you desire and what you do are acceptable, if you feel good about yourself and truly like yourself as a sexual being. Get help if you do not.

4. Taking Responsibility

Above all, take responsibility for your own sexual behavior. It is an important part of your life, and your life is your responsibility. Also take responsibility for the fact that there are probably some aspects of your sex life that you are ashamed or embarrassed to disclose. Recognize that most people have some secret, due to society's conditioning that sex is "dirty." If sex is in any way shameful to you, get professional help. If you are obsessed with sex, or truly phobic, or practicing perversions or unhealthy or unnatural sex that makes you uncomfortable and guilty, get help before you literally get caught with your pants down. If you are having sexual problems with your partner, go into therapy. Most of these therapies are technique-based, quite simple to utilize, and usually fast and very effective. If you are victimizing someone as part of your sexual pleasure, accept that you, too, are a victim of your own insecurities and your weak ego. Accept that this is your problem, your responsibility, and your life that you are ruining. *Stop* hurting the victim. *Stop* your behavior. Get help. There is plenty of help available for sexual problems and dysfunctions. Recognize that your sexual disorder is a manifestation of an even larger problem with yourself. It could be a problem of self-image, of needing to impress others or of desiring something other than sexual fulfillment as the outcome.

All of these are related to the weak ego and an extreme lack of self-esteem. The need to victimize someone sexually may be part of a personality disorder or reflect a problem with appropriate development of your conscience. These things are illnesses or disorders that require professional help. No one with this type of emotional disease can be expected to solve such severe problems alone. In these cases, getting treatment is the only sensible, sane thing to do. Manifesting illness by taking it out on others, especially those who are vulnerable or weak, moves past the realm of sickness and into being evil. While you cannot always control your pathology, you most certainly can control your behavior with others. At the very least it is in your control to seek help. Do so immediately, so that you can begin your recovery and your discovery of the good within you.

If, on the other hand, you are the victim of sexual abuse, you do not need to take responsibility for what has happened to you. Remember, you can only be responsible for something that you can control. If someone abuses you in any way, including sexually, you are not in control. It will become self-destructive if you try to blame yourself for things that are truly not your fault. Society has done grievous harm to victims of sexual abuse in the past by intimating that somehow the victim was responsible or led the perpetrator on or caused the abuse in some way. This is simply not true and reflects a simplistic and superficial view about sexual abuse. Please do not take responsibility for what was not in your control. Get help so that you can get past what has happened to you. You did not deserve it, you did not create it, and you did not *do* it. What happened was *not* your fault.

You were hurt and you will heal. You are good. No one can take that away from you.

5. Forgiving

Forgive yourself for the sexual problems you may be having. This means that you will allow yourself to move past what is holding you in a negative place. Once you have taken responsibility for what is in your control and looked for help to change, you can begin to let go when you forgive. If you have used sex for other motives in the past, you can now recognize that this is not what sex is about. Recognize that many of your erroneous concepts and negative feelings about sex are due to faulty training. If your sexual identity has been tied to your weak ego, if you have used others to validate your own sexuality, know that this is also due to your conditioning. Forgive society and others for teaching you erroneously. Forgive yourself for being such a good student of bad training. Forgive yourself for believing the stereotypes associated with sex roles. Develop a dual nature by recognizing that you have both masculine and feminine attributes and that this is an important definition of being human. Forgive yourself for focusing most of your attention on your gender and work on developing what you have ignored. In other words if you are "all male"—strong, brave, stoic, and physical—practice being vulnerable, admit your fears, express more feelings, and tend to your intuitive side. If, on the other hand, you have overworked your feminine side, try being more independent, reacting less and doing more to take care of yourself, and practice restraint with your feelings and always following your heart and intuitions. Become balanced and whole. Forgive yourself for not already being so. You did not know what you needed until now; it is easier to forgive when you realize that you cannot be perfect.

It can be very difficult to forgive the sexual abuse of children and the innocent that continually occurs. It is also very hard to forgive an entire society, including parents, teachers, and adults whom you love, for so much erroneous training in the area of sex, sex roles, and sexuality. It may indeed seem as if the entire culture is suffering. It probably is. Just separating yourself enough to perceive that there is something horribly wrong with society's way of dealing with a natural process is the beginning of your change. You do not have to follow anyone else's thinking if you do not choose to. It may be almost impossible to forgive an entire culture, society as you now know it, for the way that sex is perceived, discussed, and dealt with. It may be enough for you to let go of your needs for society's approval and to recognize that it does not care whether you approve or not.

Concentrate on forgiving yourself for your sexual limitations and for imposing your beliefs upon others. Forgive yourself for being comfortable with ideas that you really know are not correct or complete. You do not have to forgive yourself for anything you thought, said, or did (that did not intentionally hurt anyone else) if you did not know when you did it that it was wrong or hurtful. In other words, what you were doing, thinking, saying, even feeling is what you were trained to do, and your training is not your fault. Up to this point, that is. Now you have an understanding that there is both more and less to what you have previously learned. There is more to you than the limitations imposed by being one sex. There is less to the actual act of sex than society has led you to believe. Sex is paradox: more simple than you have been trained to know, yet more mysterious than you will ever discover. Your sexuality involves much more than your physical appearance. Forgive yourself for spending so much time worrying about your looks. Forgive yourself for concentrating entirely on the externals and for neglecting or denying your internal self. Forgive yourself, but do not stop here. Move on, move ahead, move around, but above all, move inside.

When you have been sexually victimized, you will probably want to be able at some point to forgive the abuser, so that you can really let go and emotionally move away from what has happened. This process is not simple and cannot occur too quickly, or it will be superficial and may even lead to more pain for the victim. When you have been hurt in any way, you will need time to heal. You will need extra love and support and attention, beginning with what you give yourself. You will need to lower your expectations about being strong, being stoical, rising above what has happened. You will need to go through the other steps completely before you can think about forgiveness. Please get professional help to get you through this process. There are many supportive, trained individuals who deal with victims every day. Do not try to heal alone; you do not have to. Forgive yourself for not being superhuman and for not knowing all the answers.

Finally, forgive others for not always taking care of your

sexual needs. They cannot do so, just as they cannot always take care of any of your other needs. Just because someone loves you does not mean that he (or she) will always be able to make love to you. Forgive him for not knowing what you want in bed. After all, you do not always know exactly what you want. Forgive him when he does not want you or wants you too much. Recognize that this has much more to do with where he is at the moment than with who you are. Let him be. Take care of your own sexual needs yourself when your partner is uninterested or unavailable. Learn that forgiveness is essential to a healthy relationship in the sexual area as well as in all other aspects of the relationship.

6. Appreciating

If you have followed the other steps and discovered that it is really all right to be sexual, you will love this step. For now you get to thank God for being a sexual being. You get to begin learning that sex is fun, the sexual act with someone you love can cover a multitude of experiences, from pure joy to wild and crazy, from risk taking to quietly comfortable. Sex with someone you love is good, even when it is not great. It can lead to the feeling of oneness with the universe. You can practice rejoicing in your own sexuality and express yourself to yourself and to others as a complete sexual being. You can greatly appreciate that, in order to do all this, you do not have to change one thing about your external body. You really do not have to lose those ten or more pounds, you do not have to see a plastic surgeon, or buy expensive clothes or work out in the gym all the time. Just as you are right now you are sexual. If you are breathing, you are sexual. It is not your potential, it is the reality of living.

Appreciate the simplicity of the idea that being sexual is recognizing your own worth, internal beauty, and goodness. The concept is simple; the practice can be incredibly difficult. You may never do this, or anything, perfectly, but you can begin by appreciating that you want to begin. You probably know instinctively that society is wrong about sex. You can appreciate that this is not your mistake and you do not have to follow along blindly. Your beauty is not determined by society's (Madison Avenue advertising) definitions of beauty. You do not have to sell yourself or buy anything from others. You can be free of all the hype and you can deprogram yourself, just by focusing on what is inside you rather than what is outside anyone else. Appreciate that this process, though difficult, is not complicated and that it is the only thing that will truly work, no matter what anyone else does or thinks. Your perception of yourself as sexual is entirely in your own control. Your awareness of your inner beauty is your life work. When you discover it, so will others. Then you will have great sex, exude sexuality, practice sensuality, and experience great fun.

7. Rewarding

The previous few lines sound as if they are all the rewards that you will ever need or want. And ultimately they will be. Along the way, however, while you are discovering your own sexuality for yourself, shedding sex-role limitations, practicing being whole, balanced, and complete, you can reward yourself for your efforts, even though you have not completed your progress. Begin rewarding yourself when you begin trying. Reward yourself when you are confused, when you are hurt, and when everything seems to be too much work. Reward yourself for surviving. That is no mean feat. Reward yourself for recognizing that you are sexual even if you do not always believe it. The best reward of all, ever, is to tell yourself that you love your Self. Other good rewards are a pat on the back (yes, you can physically pat yourself), a smile in the mirror, a compliment given to your Self, a small gift, perhaps of time for yourself or of something you really want that is only for you.

If you have been obsessed with your body image and consequently have a love-hate relationship with food, do not use food as a reward. You can reward yourself with food only if you have no guilt or shame or remorse for doing so. Food may be associated with your body image, which then correlates it to your feelings of sexuality. When you work on your sexuality and internal self-image by focusing on self-esteem concepts and practices, food becomes just food, in the same way that sex becomes just sex.

Reward yourself for jumping off society's model about sex, expanding your repertoire, letting go of unrealistic expectations, and discovering the critical difference between your sexuality and the act of sex. Especially reward yourself when you search for the similarities among both sexes. Reward yourself for being human, for being sexual, for loving sex, and for loving your Self in this incredibly sexual-spiritual world.

VII ⌁ *The Chosen Family*

At a certain time in our lives we feel the urge to "nest." We respond to this biological conditioning by wanting to "settle down," have a family, develop some roots. We decide to get married, or live together as if we were married, for a variety of reasons, some of which are healthy and some of which are not. We can recognize the difference between these reasons if we are mature, secure, and emotionally independent. But when we are not these things, the chances for creating a healthy marital relationship are considerably lessened. Unfortunately this biological urge to marry and the societal pressure to respond to it usually occur when we are still quite young, at a time when very few of us have the experience necessary to know who we are, what we want, or how to be secure within ourselves.

The Marital Myth

Our reasons for getting married set the stage for what will happen in the future relationship; they provide the foundation and usually determine the success of the partnership and the eventual outcome. In our society we have been taught that the critical element in the marital relationship is *love*. We have been raised on fairy tales and stories with happy endings, which share that wonderful concept of being loved. Time and again we have been told that love makes things right; we can solve any difficulties and surmount any hurdles if we have love. We believe that finding the one love that exists for us—our soul mate, our Mr. or Mrs. Right—will ensure our own happy ending. We love this romantic myth, and notwithstanding all the evidence to the contrary, most of us seek it at some level for our salvation, happiness, and well-being.

We choose or are chosen by one of our lovers and become a couple. We surmount our fears of intimacy and succumb to our dependencies and fears of loneliness. Most often we are elated because we think we are beginning our own happily-ever-after story. We are no longer single but are now part of a recognized pair, and as such we think we have found the answers to some of our most basic problems. We are usually more than willing to give up whatever independence we have in order to gain security, safety, and a sense of belonging. It is amazing how many of us enter into marriage believing that our most dominant fears and needs will now be resolved. As if going through a rite of passage—marriage or cohabitation—by itself will change our most primitive fears—abandonment and loneliness, loss and insecurity.

The Problem with Love

We usually enter marriage by equating love with passion, excitement, sexual interest, and need. We believe or hope that, in our case, this will always last. We also want our partner always to provide us with the same comfort, happiness, and safety that we now feel, and we are convinced that we will never again really be lonely. After all, isn't that what marriage is for? Now that there are two of us, together we can stand anything. As long as we are united, we can face the world and conquer any problems. "United we stand, divided we fall" seems to be the appropriate motto for this relationship. And of course all of this feels good and natural and right, in the beginning.

It is only much later, when the marriage is in crisis, that we begin to doubt and question the validity of these initial concepts. For most of us it takes time for the illusions to shatter. We have to learn for ourselves (we simply do not learn from the examples of other couples) that first love, the romantic kind, changes or disappears. Everybody "knows" that this is going to happen, but most of us do not really believe it will happen to us. In the marital relationship we never seem to question exactly how we are going to know to do it differently than others. We fail to consider that we have all been trained from the same model and are all subject to its shortcomings.

Therefore when the illusions are gone and the initial feelings of love have changed, we are just as frustrated and confused as everyone else. Our great passion has been replaced by familiarity or, even worse, apathy. Our comfort has changed to boredom, and our excitement has been replaced by frustration and anger. The great need we once had to always be with our beloved and to spend every possible moment with this marvelous, exciting, interesting person has now become a driving need to change our spouse into someone else. This situation is so normal and prevalent that most of us can easily recognize ourselves and our marriages in the jokes, stereotypes, situation comedies, movies, and songs with this theme. Sometimes we can even laugh at ourselves when we do recognize the similarities to our behavior. Most often, unfortunately, we do not perceive our marital situation as funny.

The Marital Script

Many of us begin our marriages determined not to repeat the patterns of our own family of origin; we desire to do things differently, to do things better. We are convinced that we will not make our parents' mistakes. Often we do not realize until too late that we are products of these early patterns and that, as human animals, we repeat what we know. Most of us assume that there are really only two choices on how to do marriage: (a) we can copy our parents and select partners who remind us of them and then do what they did; or (b) we can choose partners who are nothing like our parents and do exactly the opposite from how we were raised. When we think that these are our only choices, we fail to realize that in both cases our life is being directed by a script written by others. When we imitate our parents, we are following the overt script. When we do the exact opposite, we are following the antiscript, which means we are still allowing the script to direct us, but now it is in the opposite direction. In neither case are we directing our own lives, making our own choices and being true to ourselves. How many of us are appalled to discover we treat our partners as we saw our parents treat each other? How often do we find ourselves saying or doing the same kinds of hurtful things we heard our parents say and do?

The Model for Marriage

Recognizing ourselves in others and discerning that we are repeating the patterns we learned in our original families indicate that we are following what we have been taught. Our training, society's model for marriage, has led us to the same kinds of problems that most everyone else seems to be experiencing. This can be a critical revelation because it indicates that we have been good students of a bad model rather than failures at marriage. One of the major problems with the way we have learned to regard marital relationships is the lack of a healthy long-term model. Most of our role models for marriage are short-term excitement and long-term difficulty. When we do look for long-term models of good marriages, we find that romantic love, as defined above, is not the critical element of the relationship. It has been replaced by kindness, respect, and appreciation. These qualities then lead to good communication, feelings of safety, security, and belongingness. This in turn leads to a different kind of love, a lasting and deep commitment to the Self and to the other. Aren't these the very things we hoped to achieve in our marriage to begin with? Even though our training may not have taught us how to have a life-lasting relationship, we can still learn how to do so.

Love Is Active

We can begin with the concept that love is something we do rather than something we feel. In doing so, by making love an activity rather than a state, we immediately gain some control over the situation. We cannot control how we feel, how others feel, or what others do, but we can control what we do and how we behave. We can forget about measuring or re-creating the early stage of romantic love, and we can focus instead on being kind. There is never too much kindness; being kind is not something to do occasionally. As with self-esteem, it is process and needs constant practice. When we are actively striving to be kind, when we consistently choose to be kind rather than to be hurtful, rude, critical, or aggressive, we really do become kind. What we practice becomes what we are. We are good—that is a given—but we have to choose to reveal this goodness through our activities. Doing our goodness is our choice and probably our life's work. Being kind becomes doing good. This is not the same thing as being "nice" because niceness is usually generated from trying to please others in order to be esteemed by them. True kindness comes from the inner self, as only we can recognize the choice we are making. Only we know that it may often be easier to succumb to being unkind and that it can be much more difficult to choose kindness, especially to our spouse who is not always kind to us. We have learned to focus on what the other is doing to us; reverse this and look at what we are doing. We cannot change the other, but we can change ourselves. Paradoxically, by changing our own behavior, by choosing kindness rather than criticism and pain, we model for our partners how we would like to be treated. This, then, makes it easier for them to change and practice kindness to us.

Another way to love actively is to be respectful of the one we love. Everyone has something that can be respected; hopefully we would not marry someone if there were not some qualities that we admire, like, and enjoy. Showing respect is the activity of verbalizing and recognizing these positive attributes in the other. When we give honest compliments and openly acknowledge these qualities and talents in our mate, we also allow the partner to recognize his or her own goodness and worth. This is encouragement, and it is a critical element of the strong, healthy, committed relationship. It then becomes easy to appreciate what we respect and to show our appreciation to the spouse. Again, we are modeling what we would like to receive from our partner and in a very real sense we are teaching him or her how to treat us in the way we most want to be treated. We are actively creating a relationship that works rather than passively waiting for one to happen.

Of course being kind, respectful, and appreciative of a partner requires that the partner has the capability of reciprocating. If we are being kind to someone who abuses us, or showing respect to a tyrant, or being appreciative of destructive tendencies, we are functioning as a martyr and a codependent. In order not to be part of a dysfunctional relationship, we must begin with the premise that we ourselves are worthy of kindness, respect, and appreciation. When we recognize this, then we will no longer allow ourselves to be scapegoated or victimized. If we are in such a situation, our recognition of self-worth will allow us to get out and stop the abuse. It is critical for us to recognize that we cannot actively love another unless we can actively love ourselves. Similarly we cannot actively be loved by those who are unable to love themselves. We cannot change their perception of themselves (only they can do that), but we can focus on changing our feelings about our Self. We can also change our own behavior. It is easier to do so when we start with the premise that we are first worthy of our own love and then worthy of our partner's love. This recognition allows the partner to do the same—first have self-love and then have love for us.

The Reality of Change

Another attribute of a good long-term relationship is the recognition that change will occur but that this change cannot be controlled or regulated by the couple. In other words change is inevitable, but the manner and outcome of this change is a mystery. This is a fact that is often ignored or unrecognized by most of us. Many years ago Ann Landers wrote a column about a couple on their wedding day and how they each perceived the other in the future. The husband looked at his wife and projected her ahead looking and acting exactly as she was on this day. She remained young, slender, and adoring. The wife, on the other hand, saw her husband in the future as mature, wise, middle-aged-handsome, and distinguished, largely due to her own efforts at remaking him. Unfortunately there is much truth in these perceptions. One partner is completely denying the possibility of change and the other is trying to control the direction of it. Neither of these perceptions is possible.

Because we cannot control change (except in ourselves and then only to some degree), the only realistic and healthy response to the reality that everything and everyone changes is to let others be who they are. Let the other be. How very simple that sounds and yet how incredibly difficult that is to do. The secret to letting others be is to focus our energies for change onto ourselves. When we are trying to force others to change, when we are trying to project our needs onto them, we are ignoring the indications that our own needs and wants are not being met. It is an interesting phenomenon that when we are irritated, frustrated, and unhappy with our spouses, we are often projecting our own feelings of insecurity onto them. If we can recognize what is happening and learn to refocus our attention from them onto our Self, we can avoid many unhappy, unhealthy, and discouraging times in our marriages.

Marriage: State Versus Process

Marriage in and of itself is not the solution to any problem that we bring into the conjugal relationship. Our perception of marriage is that it is a state, just as external to the self as the ring that signifies the marriage. We cannot expect a ring to be an active force for change, and yet too many of us expect the state of marriage to be just that. The reality is that marriage is process, ongoing, ever-changing, and only as healthy as the two participants are. Marriage becomes what we create and put in instead of what we expect and take out. It is logical and realistic to recognize that one person with problems plus another with problems equals two people with twice the problems. However, our illusions about marriage are so strong and prevalent that most of us believe we can add the two people, but subtract the problems. Or at the very least most of us enter marriage believing that being together will lessen our difficulties. How many of us enter this conjugal state aware that we have now added significantly to our repertoire of problems?

There are few guarantees in life, but one of them is that any unresolved problems with the Self will become marital problems. Also any submerged or unrecognized problems with the Self will surface and be clearly acknowledged by the spouse. Marital therapies and marital counselors abound and continue to grow as this truth becomes openly recognized. Two damaged and problematic people make for a damaged and difficult marriage. Because life consists of problems and no one is free of them, it makes sense that marriage is also about problems. It provides us, then, with one of our greatest settings in which to become problem solvers. Life, marriage, and problem solving are all process. When we focus on the process instead of being overwhelmed by the content or context, we can begin to perceive our problems as challenges. We can recognize that we are learning and growing and becoming skillful; we can share our skills with our partners and allow them to help us in our times of need. We can recognize that healthy, strong, close marriages come from adversity, solving difficulties, and accepting the realities of life. Our marriage can then parallel our personal search for meaning, growth, and wholeness. It can parallel but never become the search. When we are able to change our expectations about marriage and accept the realities, we can then begin to encounter the closeness, intimacy, connection, and comfort we originally sought. Marriage, as state, cannot provide these things. Marriage, as process, as part of our own individual journey, can become these things, but only after we have discovered that our serenity can only be found within the inner self.

Becoming a Parent

When we are unable to perceive our marriage as process and seem to be stuck in the problems, or when we realize that our spouse cannot provide us with the comfort, love, and security we need, we often seek our fulfillment by having a child. When a marriage is troubled, one of the most unfortunate solutions seems to be to have a baby. Having a child, we believe, will give the marriage a common ground. Parenthood will provide the stability and perhaps even the security the marriage lacks. We think that the baby will cement the marriage. If one and one cannot provide two happy people, let's try for three! This is of course a worst-case scenario. However, it is also one that occurs frequently.

Again we can look to our training as one of the reasons for this. We are taught that procreating is a major reason for being married, and our biological urges, combined with societal pressures, reinforce this illusion that children make marriages happy. In spite of research to the contrary—that marital satisfaction decreases with the birth of the first child and remains depressed until the last child leaves the home—we continue to foster the illusion of marital bliss as being enhanced by babies. We love the myth, hate the reality, and tend to believe that we can do it differently than everyone else.

But suppose the marriage is good; it is working for both partners, and the time has come to enlarge and enrich the family circle. Both spouses have taken a realistic appraisal of themselves and have been able to support each other and work through their difficulties in a healthy manner. Both are aware that they do not "need" to have a baby in order to save the marriage. They are mature adults and realize that an infant will not solve their problems. The foundation for parenthood is healthy, and it seems realistic to assume that enlarging the family will bring fulfillment and happiness. To these couples it is often a great shock when they discover that they have added a completely new set of dynamics to their marriage. Because they have effectively worked through some of the difficulties involved in being married, they naturally tend to assume that they can easily handle the problems of parenthood. All too frequently happy couples quickly become stressed, frustrated, and unhappy parents with some moments of great joy but many more of difficulties.

Patterns and Expectations

Even if we consciously try to raise our families differently from the way we were raised, all too often we find ourselves confronting the same problems. It is almost as if there is a cosmic script out there and we are following the same cues and responding with the same lines and actions. Even if we do not communicate with our partner as our parents communicated with each other, even if we have learned from our parents' mistakes, we may discover that parenthood brings out in us the same patterns that we hated as a child. How, we wonder, has this happened?

Being a parent, we know, is serious business. Most of us start out with good intentions, high expectations, and a firm resolve to be a wonderful parent. We bring that helpless bundle home from the hospital and make lots of promises to ourselves: *I will always love this child. I will never hurt it. I will learn from my own childhood. I will be there for this baby, and as it grows up, I will be patient and objective. I will listen and I will explain. I will curb my temper. I will change for this child!* And if we do not have such expectations for ourselves, we find we do have some for the child: *This child will always love me. This child will make me proud. I will finally have a close, sharing relationship with someone who is mine. Now I have a reason for living and for doing my best. This child has changed my life!*

The Reality of Parenting

All of our expectations for ourselves and our child seem well founded when things are going well. When the baby is little and cute, when we have mastered the art of feeding and diapers and have relaxed enough to realize that the infant can survive in spite of our mistakes, it is easy to believe that we have realized our expectations. But all too soon the difficulties surface. To begin with, there is never enough time. Babies take all the time we seem to have and then some. The primary caretaker, usually the mother, knows how ravenously infants gobble up time. The other spouse may recognize this and may share in the duties, thereby losing much of his "free time." Taking care of a child always means having less time to take care of ourselves and having little to no time for the spouse. Energy is also eaten up by this incredibly demanding, hungry, wet, and utterly charming little new person. Time to pursue other interests is severely curtailed as the most interesting thing in our lives becomes this rapidly changing little being. Money frequently becomes a problem, as the equipment, medical expenses, clothes, diapers, food, and toys for the baby can be exorbitant. When both parents work, the problems of time, energy, and money geometrically increase, as the cost of infant and child care is very high. With absolute certainty the primary caretaker has changed and functions as a different person. This means that the marriage has changed and the couple's life is very different.

Reemerging Problems

Some of us discover our old problems of insecurity and dependency, fear of intimacy and immaturity, early on in the parenting process. Some of us become jealous of the time and attention the child receives from the other parent, the one who used to dote on us. Some of us become possessive of the child and want exclusive love and admiration from it. We want the child to belong to us and no one else; we have finally found our worth and position here. The rest of the world, including our spouse, can take a backseat. And some of us unfortunately discover that having a child does not cause us to love ourselves and that we have added one more problem to our lives rather than solving our basic problem of lack of self-love. A few of us may even discover that we are incapable of really loving another, even a helpless and dependent child. We feel that another weight has been added to our overburdened lives. Instead of solving any problems or enhancing our marriage, this baby has brought back many of the issues we thought were over when we undertook becoming a couple and, later, becoming a parent. Instead of feeling more loved, we feel stretched to the wire. Instead of feeling happy, we feel tired and frustrated. And instead of bringing us closer to our partners, we often feel alienated from them. These feelings can be quite similar to the feelings of the hopeless child—that there is never enough for him or her—and to the confused adolescent—whatever is done seems to be wrong.

Responsibility Without Control

We all too soon discover that "our" child becomes his (or her) own person, with ideas and beliefs and actions that are outside of our control. This child is clearly and often painfully separate from us. He embarrasses us, does not follow orders, and does not make our lives easier. What has happened to those great expectations we had? We find that we are either blaming ourselves once again for not doing something exactly right or that we are blaming others—the child, the spouse, the world—because things have not worked out as we envisioned. We are back in the blame game and may shock ourselves by what we hear coming out of our mouths, or by doing things that we swore we would never do. We may find ourselves acting, talking, and thinking as our parents did when we were small.

One of the critical reasons we are always going to have problems when we have children is that in this situation the rule that we do not have responsibility for what we cannot control is not applicable. In this case, with our dependent children, we do have total responsibility, but we do not have complete control. We are responsible for their survival, for nurturing and protecting them, for teaching them what they need to know, for providing them with security and safety, for loving them, attending to their needs, and disciplining their behavior. We have to do for them all the things that we are hopefully learning to do for ourselves, and we have to do these things for them even if we have not yet learned to take care of ourselves. This can be really difficult! We need to be responsible parents even though our children are not in our total control. We quickly recognize that our children, even when they are tiny infants, are not under our control. They cry at inappropriate times, misbehave when we most want them to behave, say embarrassing things in front of others, demand attention when we are pressed for time, and constantly create new problems for us to solve.

Being Flexible

When we have responsibility without control, we are compounding the difficulties inherent in learning to let go. We begin our relationships with our children with a great deal of power over them, but gradually, as they grow, we have to relinquish some of this power in order for them to learn, develop, and become independent beings. This can be very difficult, as there are no hard-and-fast rules about how or when to let go. It may help for the parent to think of an imaginary elastic band between him and the child. In the beginning this elastic band is very short, and the parent and child are very closely tied together. By the age of two the band is long enough for the child to begin to explore his world and briefly venture away from the parent, but also short enough for the child to get back quickly to the safety of the parent. Think of this elastic band as an analogy for the attachment process. If the parent lets go of this band, the child feels abandoned. If the parent holds on to it too tightly, the child feels constrained and unable to develop normally. As the child grows up, the band also grows longer and the parent allows more exploration and adventure to occur.

Sometimes the child will want more flexibility than the band allows, and this will cause tension and discomfort. Sometimes the child will snap back too quickly, as in the example of running back to the parent rather than exploring the environment; this occurs when the child is overattached. Sometimes the parent will pull too hard and not allow the child necessary exploration and interaction with others; this is the case of the overattached parent. Both of these situations will cause conflict and pain. But this is a flexible process in which everyone is constantly learning and pain and adjustment are part of this natural process. It is not easy to know how much flexibility the child needs, as this is not determined by what the child wants or what the parent wants. Some compromise needs to be given on both sides. When we, as parents, demonstrate flexibility along with concern for our children, we are modeling future behavior for them to demonstrate toward us. The most important thing the parent can do, the one thing that will override the many mistakes parents naturally make, is always to let the child know that there is a connection and that the child can always return to safety and love. This is the ultimate responsibility for all parents to give to their children—the love, attention, and security that are the child's basic rights.

The Importance of Time

One of the clear problems in today's society is the lack of time and the stress this generates. This seems to be particularly relevant in the parenting years. And time is one of the most critical variables that we need to give to our children. It simply takes time to be a good parent. It takes time to listen to our children, play with them, help them solve their own problems, and show affection and love. It takes time to be with the child, and being is what it is really all about. The child can be one of the great teachers of the art of being, having fun, simplifying and enjoying life. But we cannot learn these lessons when we are too busy working, running errands, watching television, or trying to do chores. This is not to say that we need to spend every hour of every day with our child; we also err when we make the child the center of our lives and let our existence revolve around this little being. This issue of time is another continuum, with too much and too little—the end points—causing the major problems. We can be flexible here, giving more time when we can and less when we have no choice, but the important variable is that we make the time we spend with our children a top priority in our lives.

As our children grow, we quickly discover that the amount of time they need with us diminishes drastically once they discover the power of peers. It seems to be another paradox that just when our children are becoming really good company for us and people that we truly enjoy being with, they tend to prefer the company of their friends. When they are little and demanding and a lot of work, they cannot bear to be parted from us. Remember, children are not here to make our lives easy or to help us feel fulfilled; they are not here to satisfy our expectations or live up to our illusions. They are here to begin their own journeys through life and to discover who they are, what they want, and how to also become heroes in this difficult world.

The Second Decade

Most of us do realize that our children are not going to make things easier for us as they get older. As a matter of fact, when they become adolescents, things are generally going to go from bad to worse. If the child's job is to tease us into confronting our own problems, the adolescent's can be described as bludgeoning us with our own shortcomings and mistakes. It is almost as if we have been hiding ourselves under a rock and the adolescent feels the need to remove the rock and expose us in our vulnerable and frightened state to the entire world. Can the adolescent remove the rock gently and compassionately? Hell, no! This adolescent, our own creation, in order to rebel against us and to find himself, feels compelled to discover all our weaknesses and faults, all our problems, and to throw them back at us as justification for the rebellion.

It is true that the period of adolescence has become more difficult than it used to be—more difficult for society, for the teenager, and certainly for the family. While it has always been a difficult time (read the Greeks for their discussions about this!), the lessening in importance of our institutions—such as church, state, and school—and the lessening in strength of the family system have certainly contributed to problems during this decade. Additionally the attention given by the media to this age group, and the amount of money spent by adolescents has given them premature and perhaps unwarranted economic power. Many teenagers are spending their parents' money without the parents having any say in the process. Thus, adolescents are exhibiting control while parents have the actual responsibility. This unbalance often becomes a source of tremendous conflict.

The Adolescent Personality

At this point it may be helpful for the parent to think of the adolescent as having a decade-long personality disorder. The symptoms of this include not developing a clear sense of identity; he (or she) simply does not know who or what he is. He also does not know exactly what he wants, nor what the reasons are for wanting these things. The favorite answer to anything during adolescence is probably "I don't know." As parents we can take this literally. The adolescent has rapid mood swings and can go from elation to depression within minutes. There is tremendous anger and it is usually inappropriately expressed. This is a time of narcissism, when "me" is the most important consideration. He also has difficulty with criticism, needs constant attention, approval, and admiration, is preoccupied with the self, has unrealistic fantasies, can be interpersonally exploitative, and is frequently jealous of others. These characteristics are not considered part of a disorder because they are developmentally appropriate during this decade. It is part of the process of learning about the Self and learning what to keep and what to give up with others. The above traits become a disorder after the adolescent matures and does not change this way of thinking and behaving.

As difficult as adolescence is to both the teenager and the

parent, this period will be intolerable to the parent who has not matured and come to grips with himself (or herself). The parent who is suffering the same symptoms will hardly be able to tolerate them in the child. The person who has not yet resolved the problems of the family of origin will find it extremely difficult to deal with them in another member of the family. One major difference here is that the adolescent is being developmentally appropriate, while the parent is developmentally delayed. There is no easy way out; sooner or later life forces us to deal with our difficulties with relationships.

Flexibility Again

If we remember the analogy of the elastic band for the child, it may be helpful to change it in adolescence to the bungee (that big, long cord to which people are attached and thrown off bridges or high places just for the thrill of it). Just as there is an element of danger and self-destruction in bungee jumping, so also is there in adolescence. Teenagers today face a tremendously difficult world, one in which simply staying alive seems to have become a major concern. While we, as parents, may still perceive them as our little ones, they themselves are trying to cope as grown-ups without possessing the necessary skills or experience to do so. In the analogy to the bungee, the parent must function as the safe, stable, solid end to which the bungee is attached. It is not fun to be the mainstay, the point of attachment, when we do not have any control over what is going on at the other end. It can feel like a disaster when we are afraid of what our children are throwing themselves into. And yet we must remain stable, secure, and attached. If the adolescent does not have this safety to return to (even when he adamantly denies needing it), if we let go of our end, the adolescent will feel alienated, may emotionally regress, stop developing, and will certainly be vulnerable to self-destruction and dangerous peer influences.

Parents have one great advantage in the conflict with their teenage children—an advantage that is often overlooked. We, as parents, have been where they, as teens, are now. They have not yet been where we are. We survived adolescence, we made it through those insecure, often lonely, confused years and we became adults. Our advantage exists only if we can remember what it was like during that time—how we felt and what we did and some of the craziness and self-destructive things we attempted. This is no time for the parent to develop amnesia about a whole decade of his (or her) own life. This is exactly the time to walk down memory lane and remember, remember, remember. Then take these memories and try to perceive the Self at exactly the age of our adolescent. By putting ourselves in their places, we can better perceive the world through their eyes and begin to understand where they are coming from, what they are feeling, and how we can share our similarities with them. Then we can start to communicate with them and make it easier for them to trust us.

Modeling good parenting is not the same as playing the role of the "good" parent. When we think that parents have to be a certain way and we forget that once we, too, were crazy kids, we close doors of communication with our children. It is true that none of this is easy, and more often it is painful, frustrating, and seemingly unrewarded. It may help to remember that if our children learn, if our adolescents survive and mature, if we ourselves do not go crazy in the process, then all of us have done a good job. If we are truly doing the best we can, then it is enough.

Stepparenting

If we recognize that two parents dealing with their biological child can have many difficulties and problems to resolve, it becomes much easier to understand the reality that coping with stepchildren can be a heroic task. As the numbers of divorces increase, the numbers of blended families also grow, and having stepchildren is no longer a rare event. This may indeed be the case where adding two parents plus one child equals not three sets of problems but at least four or five and, quite likely, more. The stepchild comes into the relationship with another parent and his or her numerous relatives, all of which are external to the marriage. All these people do not belong in the marital relationship, but they most certainly do belong to the child. At best we are going to have a complicated and often controversial situation in which to raise this child. At worst we are going to have disaster. For the child's sake the parent and stepparent will have to consciously work at minimizing the stress of dealing with all these people. They need to try to keep that burden off the stepchild's shoulders. This will never be an easy task and at times it may be an impossible one, but it is a necessary job for the adults in the family to undertake. Keeping the relationships with the child's extended family and other parent as civil and workable as possible will alleviate a great deal of suffering and unnecessary pain for the stepchild. It will keep this child from attempting to do an adult's job, either that of peacemaker or that of feeling responsible and guilty. Learning to accept, to let go, to take responsibility only for what we can control, and to express our feelings will help us in this difficult situation of dealing with the unchosen ones in our chosen family.

As difficult as these external (outside the marriage) problems may be, they will be nothing compared with the internal problems between the biological parent and the stepparent who have not established basic guidelines for parenting. The stepparent may be placed in an untenable situation in which he or she is given responsibility for the stepchild without having any control. When a child is born to us, we do not question our rights to control. However, when the child is part of a package deal, and not of our complete choosing, we do not have any control unless our spouse, the natural parent, allows us to share his or her control. In situations where the other biological parent is not a factor, these control issues tend to be more similar to that of the natural family. However, in most cases, the child may have four parents, all of them with different degrees of control. When the stepchildren are small, these difficulties are usually more easily resolved than when they are prepubescent or adolescent, for obvious reasons.

Stepparenting an adolescent who resents, rebels, and is consistently rude and disrespectful to his unchosen stepparent is surely hell on earth! Trying to parent this stepmonster without the support and cooperation of the parent only compounds this hell and can quickly destroy the marital relationship. In order to avoid or change this no-win situation, both spouses need to be very clear and to agree completely on how much control the stepparent has over the stepchild. This degree of control, then, is exactly proportional to the amount of responsibility the stepparent assumes. All permutations of this correlation between control and responsibility are possible, from being a complete authority figure, to being an objective friend with small degrees of control, to being an outside party to the parenting process with no control or responsibility at all. All of these roles, and everything in between, can work if the spousal relationship is consistently clear and supportive of the roles of each in the parenting process. Making these decisions, clarifying the roles, and remaining respectful and supportive of each other throughout the parenting years can function in a very healthy way for the marital couple. Solving the challenges of stepparenting can provide an excellent model for solving the problems of life. The difficulties of stepparenting may be great, but they provide the challenge that then becomes the opportunity for personal growth.

Adoption

By the time an adoption has occurred, we may no longer think of it in terms of a problem. This is because the decision to adopt and the process of finally getting the adopted child into the home feel as if we have already solved the difficulties and hurdles along the way. This process is usually not an easy one, neither to decide upon nor to complete. Where the adoption can become a major difficulty for the parents is when the child, generally during adolescence, desires a reconnection with the birth parents. This can be compounded if the adolescent is in the rebellion phase of development and nothing the adoptive parents have done or are doing seems to be right or enough. The child can then turn family life into hell if he (or she) fantasizes that the biological parents are the perfect ones or the ideal and the adoptive parents are the enemy. This can be incredibly painful to deal with for all concerned.

One of the great blessings of having an adopted child is that we tend to accept this child as it is, without the illusions and expectations that we often place on our biological child. If we are not secure within ourselves, as so few of us are when we become parents, it is too easy to perceive our genetic offspring as the ideal or perfect parts of ourselves. Therefore we put a lot of our own baggage on this tiny new baby. It is easier not to do that with the chosen child, not of our genes. And all too often our biological babies do not look or act or feel as we imagined they would during those nine long months of pregnancy. When we adopt, we are spared this illusion-building-and-then-destroying process. We do not have to deal with it early on with adoption, but we may have to deal with painful problems when the adolescent faces his identity crisis. This problem can be reframed into a life challenge if we are able to recognize that what is happening to our intact family, what looks like possible denial or destruction to the system we have built, is instead a normal and healthy occurrence for the adopted adolescent. It is true that not all adopted children feel the need to search for their roots; it is also true that when they do, it is not a renunciation of the parents who have raised them. It may feel like it, but usually the adopted child will come to the realization that parenting is not the same as procreating. This awareness often leads to more appreciation for and closeness with the adoptive family. When we ourselves are mature, healthy, emotionally stable, and able to fill our own needs for recognition and rewards, we are better able to deal with our adolescent's search for identity, be he adopted or biological. We can only do the best we can, and when we have done that, as parents or in any role in life, then we can let go, trust, and hope. Paradoxically when we are able to do these things, our problems are lessened and our solutions seem easier.

The Adult Child

We have raised our teenagers; they have survived this difficult decade and have become young adults. We may think our problems are over, but problems are never over. What has happened is that now we get to experience different kinds of problems and to face new challenges. When we remember that we only spend twenty years or so being parents of children and the rest of our lives being parents of adult children, it is amazing that so little focus has been given to this adult-to-adult relationship. The general assumption about parenting is that if we raise our children, the problems stop. The truth is that having an adult child can be one of the most difficult relationships we have, unless somewhere along the way we have learned to let go. If we have fought this process, and refused to do so, now we will be forced to let go or we will lose any chance of a healthy relationship with this adult who once was our child. The reality of this stage in our parent-child relationship is that everything that has worked before, everything that we are accustomed to doing and being, now needs to change. We can no longer have an invisible elastic band or a bungee tying us to our adult child. We can no longer maintain the role of parent that has become so familiar over the last two decades. We certainly can no longer live for our children or feel a sense of worth and esteem from being the "good" parent. Our child, who now often looks older and seems wiser than we were at his age, resents our interference and our concern. What worked before to help this same child feel safe and secure now feels like constraint or duty to him. Our adult child no longer needs us, and if we have based our lives on being needed, we will indeed feel lost. This is not our children's problem; let us try very hard not to put the responsibility for how we are feeling onto them. The last thing in the world they (or anyone else) needs, and the most alienating, is to place guilt on them for becoming separate and whole individuals.

As previously mentioned, it is an interesting and painful phenomenon to realize that the more interested we become in our children, the more we try to revolve our life around them, the less interested they are in us. At some point in our lives we must all learn about letting go. The beginning of our adult-to-adult relationship with our child is an excellent time to practice letting go. We are no longer responsible, there are no remnants left of any illusions of control, and we have no choice if we want a healthy relationship with this young adult. Let go of any needs for control. Let go of inflicting guilt as a way of keeping them attached. This absolutely does not work. Let go of the role of parent. Begin to see them in a new way. Treat them as if they were a highly respected friend. Rejoice in the freedom from responsibility. Celebrate the shedding of an old role (parent) and the beginning of a new role (friend). Once again, let go of the child, for this child has let go of childhood. Allow this new person, this young adult, created from the parents but not entirely by them, to *be*. This is not impossible if we focus on the changes that we must enact for ourselves instead of trying to keep the past relationship intact. In other words everything has changed, but all we can control, all we are now responsible for, is what we are doing. We have raised a child who is now able to take on responsibility for his or her own life and behavior. Hallelujah! Let us celebrate and go forward.

VIII ∾ Problem-Solving the Chosen Family

1. Accepting

Accept the reality of your family as it is right now. Accept the fact that your mate and your children do not function to enhance you or to solve your problems. Look at your family of choice with objective eyes. They are what they are and you are what you are. You will probably see frustration, pain, and lost hopes and ideals along with the love and the caring. Accept the fact that families are made up of flawed humans and are therefore imperfect systems. Try to discover where your family functions well and where it is dysfunctional. Almost all families have some degree of dysfunction. Accept the fact that the people you love most, the people around you, are not perfect and will never be exactly what you want them to be. Accept also that you will never be exactly what they want or need, no matter how hard you try.

Accepting eyes do not value the good over the bad; they do

not make quick value judgments. Accepting eyes look at what is there and try to see all of it in an objective, impartial way. This is very difficult, especially with the ones you love. It is even more difficult with your children. Accepting the reality of yourself and of those around you is the first and critical step toward solving problems. Remember, these can function as challenges and are not bad unless you ignore, deny, or project them on to others.

2. Letting Go

Let go of your illusions and dreams of what a family should be. Let go of the fact that something is wrong because they do not resemble what you have seen on television or in the movies. You are not Beaver Cleaver's parents, and your children are not like Beaver, nor should you or they be. Let go of comparison with others and with destructive judging. Let go of trying to be, or appearing to be, the perfect family. It doesn't work and has no basis in reality.

Stop trying to be the parent of your dreams—the one you wanted when you were a child. By now you have probably discovered that this is an impossible task. Let go of the guilt and the frustration and confusion you feel because you cannot live up to this unattainable standard. It is more than enough that you have tried to be the perfect parent because you care so much for your children. You can be parent enough without coming close to being perfect. Only perfect children need perfect parents. Since neither exist, drop the facade.

Let go of the idea that your children have to be perfect, that they have to behave, look good, be motivated, make good grades, and achieve success. For God's sake, let them be children. They are not miniature adults and they are supposed to make mistakes, do things wrong, sometimes be awful. Their job is not to make you look good. Their job is to be a child, to learn, and to grow. Their work is to play. They have plenty to do without pressure from you to do it right or better or faster. Let go of the pressure and your own projected needs for achievement.

Let go of comparisons of your child with other children, particularly the ones of your dreams. Your actual child exists; your dream child does not and will not, except in your imagination. Your actual child is not like any other in the world. This one is unique and is your reality, even though parts may not be exactly what you want. Let go of wanting the impossible.

Let go of your personal dreams, hopes, and aspirations for your child. Boy, this one is really tough! Let go of the idea that you can make him always happy. He needs some sadness, failure, frustration, disappointment, and unhappiness in order to learn, develop, and become whole. You cannot prevent these things from occurring, so let go of your desire to create such a world for your beloved little one. Let go of your dreams for this child; he will have his own dreams and aspirations. You did, you do, and if you are living someone else's dreams, you know how frustrating and unfulfilling that is to you. Allow your child to be. Do not place the burden of what you want onto such a little person.

Let go of the idea that your child has to do, to produce, to be successful. It is much more important that children are balanced and whole than that they make good grades and go to the right schools and grow up to make lots of money. An emotionally healthy child is a gift to this world and a joy to behold. An overachieving, pressured, stressed child is a symptom of a sick society. Let go of trying to make your child perfect so that he can learn to let go of the concept of perfect and enjoy being a child.

Finally, let go of the idea that this child is yours, in your control. It is more realistic to realize that he is on loan to you for a short period of time and that you will lose your babies as they grow and become their own people. Your job is not to provide a lifetime of need-fulfillment for them; your job is to provide the security and love that they need when they are little so that they can learn how to feel secure and loved when they mature.

3. Expressing Feelings

More feelings are expressed in a destructive, negative manner in the family environment than in any other milieu. Most likely you tend to take your frustrations and anger home with you and act them out. This is because you probably feel safer there than you do at work or with friends. You may have the experience of a time when your boss got mad at you and you went home and got angry with your spouse, who then yelled at the child, who kicked the dog, who then chased the cat. This may sound crazy, but it happens all too often. Anger and negativity are unfortunately easily communicated and highly contagious.

If you think of yourself as a living role model for your family, then you can learn how to express your feelings in a constructive way around the ones you most love. Explain your emotions to them as you would like them to explain theirs to you. Own your own feelings and try not to blame them on your spouse or children. Do not be afraid of negative ones. When you own whatever you are feeling, those around you will not be afraid of you. It is only when you try to make them responsible by blaming them that they become frightened. Use "I" statements: "I am angry now" or "I am feeling sad." This sounds very different from "You make me angry" or "It's your fault that I am sad."

It is important for children to know that part of life involves not feeling good or happy or confident. They need to know that there is nothing bad or wrong about anger, sadness, or confusion. The best way for them to learn this is to hear parents express these unhappy feelings. An important part of parenting occurs when the child watches parents deal with all emotions in a healthy, constructive manner. When you can express your anger without yelling at the ones you love, you are modeling a constructive expression of this emotion. When you can let go of your anger, you are teaching a valuable lesson. Children then learn that having feelings is a normal part of life and they will know how to express themselves and deal with their own disappointments in a healthy manner.

4. Taking Responsibility

Parents have almost total responsibility for their children during the first decade and continue to have it, in a diminishing fashion, during the second. They completely stop with their adult progeny, with the exception of those who are disabled.

The only one you have a lifetime responsibility toward is your own inner child. Take full responsibility for this child and for your Self. This means attending to your own needs as much as you can. It may be helpful to make a list of everything you need and to separate those things that you can do from those that others must do for you. For example you may need more affection. This you can do for yourself by saying and doing loving things to yourself. In spite of what you have been taught, self-affection really works. Try to satisfy as many of your own needs as you can and then share the ones you cannot with others, recognizing that they have the right not to comply. Allow the other members of your family to take responsibility, as they are capable of doing, for themselves. Your spouse has full responsibility for his own actions, feelings, and needs. Your adolescent has much more responsibility than your school-aged child. Your infant has none, so you must take care of him.

Take responsibility for the dysfunctional parts of your family that you can change. These are the parts that you have control over—these are your problems. You may be surprised at how many of your problems are in your own control. For example if you have negative communications and fight a great deal in your family, take responsibility for your behavior and your words. Try to stay calm and resist putting the blame on the other. Express your feelings with "I" statements and walk away when the situation is degenerating. Listen more than talk, and try to put yourself in the place of the other. Replace criticism with support as often as possible. Refocus on what you are doing rather than what is being done to you. On the other hand do not take responsibility for what you cannot control. Do not take the blame when it is not yours; do not appease others at your own expense simply to try to keep the peace. Recognize that some conflict is healthy and helps raise issues that later can be resolved.

Always take responsibility for yourself and your small children when it comes to providing safety, security, and love. You can do this for yourself, and you must do so for your little ones. If you are in danger or have abuse in your family, take charge. Get out. Change the situation. You owe this to yourself and to your children.

Taking responsibility is the opposite of blaming. It involves taking action, whereas blame keeps you in a passive, stuck state. Do not waste time on the blame game or in trying to justify why you are right and the other is wrong. Take charge, take control, take action, and change what you can.

5. Forgiving

Forgive your chosen family for not being the family of your dreams, the family of myth, the fairy-tale happily-ever-after family. Forgive yourself for not being the perfect spouse and parent. Absolve your society for creating unrealistic ideals about what the family should look like. Forgive your partner for not always being there for you; pardon yourself for not always being there for your partner. Forgive your children for not doing what you want them to do, for not being what you always want, and for not living up to your illusions. Forgive all of them for not always recognizing your good intentions toward them, your great love for them, and your desire to make their lives easier. Forgive them for not making your life easier and safer and more comfortable. Forgive yourself for not being able to do these things for them.

Forgive yourself for being impatient, unreasonable, demanding, frustrated, pushy, and overcontrolling. Then forgive your family for being the same. Forgive yourself for any abuse you may have inflicted upon your family. If it was intentional, stop doing it; then forgive yourself. If it was unintentional, pardon yourself for not knowing the harm you created, and try to do better in the future. Forgive yourself for not always knowing what you are doing and the effect it may have on those you love. Forgive them for also not knowing what they may do to you.

Yes, this is a lot to ask and very difficult to do. Forgiving is not a passive process but rather an active one that requires time, energy, and effort. It cannot be done as a mindless exercise or a vague lack of caring. Forgiveness is hard and requires much preparation. It means that you have accepted, let go, taken responsibility, expressed feelings, and are now ready and able to move on. The forgiveness you give is for you; the other may never know what you have done. It means becoming involved in the present and stopping the past from haunting you.

6. Appreciating

Your objective, accepting eyes will have seen all the good in your family. Appreciate all these things. Appreciate yourself for trying, for caring, for wanting your family to be safe and happy. Appreciate what you have done to enrich and enhance their lives: the little kindnesses and demonstrations of affection you have exhibited. Thank yourself for being there, for doing what had to be done, for caring and sharing and sometimes putting them first, above your own needs. Appreciate the fact that you sincerely try.

Now appreciate what they have done for you. Tell them how you feel, thank them for being there for you, for loving you, and for trying. Appreciate the problems that your family has encountered as vehicles toward your development and change. Appreciate the fact that the ones you live with give you the greatest challenges to overcome. Appreciate the fact that the little, everyday things that drive you crazy are the very same things that teach you patience, perspective, and the meaning of life.

7. Rewarding

You are not perfect, but you are doing your best. Reward yourself for your effort and not for obtaining your goals. Reward those in your family for trying. Often the greatest rewards in the family are verbal praise and recognition. This is especially necessary for children. Reward your children for being. Tell them you love them, are proud of them, and that you understand. Recognize the paradox: Rewarding others is most needed and beneficial during the hard times when it is the most difficult to do.

Learn that there is a huge difference between buying gifts and rewarding. Children crave affection, praise, and reinforcement much more than they need new toys or clothes. A kind word, a pat on the back, a hug and verbal expression of love are the rewards most desired in the family. Affection cannot be bought—it must be shown. A loving family exhibits loving behavior. A kind family has many acts of kindness. A healthy family is not a perfect family, but one in which all know that they are loved and valued for being themselves. The simplest way to let others know this is to tell them. Reward yourself for what you are; reward your family for what they are. In this way, you will have a happy home, one that is rewarding to all.

IX ⌒ *Separation and Divorce*

We all know the statistics; we are actively aware that love relationships are not easy and all too often end in rejection and separation. We have been inundated with news of the increase of divorce in the past decades and many of us know more divided couples than we do intact original ones. And yet when it happens to us, we are shocked. There is something wonderful and magical about the human spirit and its expectations when it comes to love. All of us have some part of ourselves that believes we will do it differently than anyone else. Most of us have high hopes when we begin our relationships that this time it will last and we will succeed. And when our relationship does not work, when we leave or are left, too many of us feel a sense of failure, about ourselves personally and about relationships in general.

The Challenge of Loss

For many of us this failure of a love relationship can be one of the most devastating trials we will ever encounter. Very few of us, if any, have the ability to perceive this time following our separation as one of our great life challenges. Most of us are engulfed with misery, loneliness, the reemergence of old fears, and the loss of hope. We truly suffer and cannot imagine ever being normal again. This seems to be one of the times when the present seems awful, the future impossible, and only the past seems relevant or positive. We hurt and we feel cheated; after all, wasn't this the relationship that was going to end the pain, stop the loneliness, and help us conquer the world? The more intensity we felt in the relationship, the more pain we will now feel. The higher the expectations, the greater the loss. And the more we have invested, the more cheated we will feel.

Emotional pain can be the most debilitating of all pains. It literally feels as if parts of ourselves, our heart or our guts, have been wrenched away and have left us with a big, gaping wound that no one else can see. This is the one time when we recognize that we are truly alone because no one else can really know how badly we feel, how much we hurt, and how isolated and separate from others we seem. Surely no one else has ever hurt this much and survived! Everyone tells us that we will recover, we will go on, we will even love again. But in our intense agony we can scarcely begin to hope that this is true. We have truly reached one of our darkest hours.

Control and Change

The amount of pain we now feel may be proportional to the amount of learning we may do. The greater the loss, the higher the likelihood for changes within ourselves and for character development. We already recognize that our world has changed, and not for the better, or we would not be in so much pain. It is very difficult to recognize that this loss we have encountered, this pain we are experiencing, this misery we are surviving is paving the way for change in us. Unlike the other changes occurring around us, we can choose the direction of our change, even though we may not be able to control very much else that is going on.

We know that we certainly cannot control our feelings; now more than ever before we are emotionally out of control in a way we have never been. We may have known that we cannot control what is happening to us; now we clearly recognize that if we could, we would not be here feeling this way. We cannot control our partner, now ex-partner, and we may feel frustrated, vulnerable, and angry that we have no power over the very person who seems to be totally in charge of our own feelings. Sometimes we may feel unable to control our own behavior and we may find ourselves doing things that we know we will regret, but we cannot seem to help it. We know we certainly cannot control the world, which seems to be continuing as if nothing of great importance had happened. We have no power to stop the large number of happy couples and young lovers who parade in front of us, sit in parks and restaurants, walk hand in hand down the street, and seem to be everywhere. All of them remind us of how lonely we are and how much a failure. We cannot control our friends, who, in trying to help us, say nasty things about our partner, the one who is causing us so much pain, the same one we once loved. All this just makes us feel more terrible. How could we have cared so much? Why are we now hurting so much over someone our friends saw through when we did not? If ever there was a time to recognize how very little control we have over anything, this is it!

The Reality About Control

The things we are now learning are life truths. What we are now seeing so clearly—how very little control we really have—is indeed one of the unrecognized realities of life. We cannot control anything except the way we feel about ourselves and the way we choose to behave. How, then, could we have felt that we had control over anything else? How did we think we had control over the way our partner felt about us and what he (or she) did? What we have now lost, and painful as it indeed is, what we are now grieving, is the *illusion of control*. When we feel loved by another, when we enter into a partnership with him, when we feel safe and secure because of his existence, we are living the illusion. Yes, it is a powerful one and one that we really want. We are not totally responsible for not recognizing that it is an illusion, because our training and our loved ones have helped to foster it. This clearly seems to be one of those lessons that we cannot learn unless we experience the reality for ourselves. And this reality can only be experienced through pain. Now that we are suffering, in great pain, alone, and once again feeling abandoned, *now* we can learn this lesson for ourselves. Granted, this is not how we would choose to learn anything, but this is how it happens. It is unfortunately true that we do not learn when we are comfortable. We only learn the important lessons about life when we are miserable, struggling, and in pain. This is the function of pain, and in the end its great blessing. We are not going through this terrible time without a reward at the end. And the best reward of all is the knowledge, experience, and challenge that come from going through the pain. We become empowered from our pain. It enables us to move on, grow, change, expand, and learn.

When we are involved in the process of pain, we cannot know about the end effects of it. When we are hurting, it is too early in the process to recognize what we will achieve by experiencing it. But we can perceive, in the midst of all the misery, that we are changing. We are not what we were before, and the darkness we are experiencing—the emotional hole in ourselves that feels as real as a physical one—will be filled again, but we will never be quite the same. Therefore the awareness of change, the experience of it, is already occurring, even though we may not like what is happening to us. The important lessons of life do not occur when we want them to, nor when we choose. Like everything else, except our own feelings and behavior, we have no control. Now that we are experiencing a life lesson, we can recognize that something good is happening, even though it may be too early to understand the relevance of it. Learning this lesson means suffering, and there is no way to learn without the pain. Therefore our present pain has a future purpose.

Choosing to Leave

If we have been the rejected one, we are clearly going to understand what has just been said. But suppose we are the one who has done the rejecting? It has been our choice to leave the relationship and we are the ones who wanted out. Even then we are going to feel some discomfort. We may not be in acute misery, we may even feel a great sense of relief, but even so we are going to be open to experiencing change. We may already be aware that rejecting another is painful, difficult, and changes the way we perceive ourselves. Many of us in this situation have experienced the pain before we left the other. By definition relationships are about sharing and caring, and somewhere along the way we discovered that we no longer wanted to do this with our partner. This realization is painful and often brings us back to the old questions of who we are and what we really want. We certainly have gone against the pressures of being nice to another (what we are doing is definitely not nice). We have encountered the fact that we are deliberately inflicting pain on someone else, someone we once cared about, in order to be free. All of this goes against our training and perhaps even against our image of ourselves. We all want to be the nice guy, the one in the white hat. Very few of us deliberately choose to be the bad guy in the black hat. Now we have been cast in that role and it is painful.

Once again we are presented with an opportunity to learn about ourselves. Our training, and societal pressure, has focused on being kind to others, taking care of them, taking responsibility for their feelings, and doing the best we can *for them*. We have gone against all this in order to leave and we may be feeling bad or that we are wrong. By definition feeling bad about ourselves is painful. Therefore we, along with our rejected partner, are in a position to learn from our experience. The harder it was to make the decision to leave, the more the opportunity for learning and growth.

The Danger of Guilt

One of the great drawbacks to learning and growing is the emergence of guilt; unfortunately this frequently occurs at the end of intimate relationships. Guilt is not a healthy emotion. As a matter of fact it is probably not a pure feeling at all, but rather a combination of a natural feeling, such as anger or sadness, with a cognitive thought or learned response. In other words guilt is a feeling that has been interpreted and expanded by the mind into another form. We demonstrate guilt when we try to explain, justify, defend, or deny our feelings because we are uncomfortable with them. We feel it when we do something that is not congruent with our self-perceptions or the way we want others to perceive us. When we think of the word *should* and all that it implies, we can quickly comprehend the cognitive component of guilt. This defeating word means that we are in opposition to ourselves or that we are being passive when we could be active. If we replace the "shoulds" with *I will* or *I won't,* we become active and in control of ourselves.

The endings of relationships are usually excellent opportunities in which to feel guilty because our training and illusions have often created unrealistic expectations for them. We have bought the myth that relationships are supposed to be forever; we have denied the reality that most of them do not last very long. In our search for that one perfect soul mate, we have tried to live a fairy tale. We want love to last forever, and when it does not, we tend to feel guilty and to take the blame for failing the myth. We are not trained to know that all our relationships are about time and place; they are all temporal and therefore temporary. The only lasting relationship that we can count on is the one with ourselves, which leads to the ultimate relationship with God. All other relationships, especially intimate ones, are rehearsals for this eternal one. If we do not believe in God, we can still understand the validity of this concept by recognizing goodness and striving for a healthy relationship with the Self, the recognition of the goodness within.

When to Leave

There are many good reasons for leaving a relationship. One of the clearest is when the relationship is not providing the ability to be true to the Self. This is most obvious in abuse situations; if we are being victimized by the partner, physically, sexually, or emotionally, we must leave in order to protect the Self from irreparable harm. Waiting for the partner to change is an exercise in futility and self-destruction. We are not responsible for the abuser's behavior—it is not our fault that he is choosing to hurt us in order to vent his own insecurities—but we are responsible for allowing him to hurt us. We are responsible for staying when we recognize that the problem is not in our control and not ours to change. We may have been trained to take care of others, but our training is crazy if we do so at the risk of our own lives and well-being. We are ultimately the only ones responsible for our own lives; we need to get out if the only other option is to get hurt.

Another good reason for leaving is when our partner does not have the ability to accept us as we really are and is constantly working on changing us into their illusion or fantasy. In other words when we are with someone who consistently and actively refuses to let us be, we need to leave. Living with someone who is always critical, jealous, possessive, unsupportive, unaffectionate, and not responsive to our true selves is a living hell. We may believe that we deserve to be treated in such a manner, but what we are experiencing are our own insecurities about our self-worth. Sometimes we may even feel that we are being "good" by allowing someone else to be so "bad"; we may get trapped in the illusion of the truly understanding and patient martyr. If so, we are stuck in living a lie and we may indeed be perpetuating the continuation of evil. We are not doing ourselves a favor by being a victim and we are not helping the other to escape the role of the evil victimizer. Leaving this kind of relationship may indeed be the beginning of change for both parties. At the very least it will be the beginning of change for the victim. True goodness in the world begins with the realization of the goodness that exists within the Self. When we are victimized, we do not allow this recognition to surface. We are not adding to the goodness of this world when we live as if we are not good and need to be punished.

When Not to Leave

There are also many reasons not to leave a relationship. When our partner is not abusing us, when this significant other lets us be who we really are, and when we are free to make our own choices and control our own lives, we may become bored or less excited or sexually uninterested. At these times we may be tempted to explore the newness of another relationship. Also when we feel unfulfilled and want someone exciting to give us a new lift in life, we may become tempted to leave. These are exactly the times when we need to turn to our internal lives instead of changing our external ones. Unfortunately we are not taught how to do so.

Instead we have been programmed to think that when romance is over, we need new lovers. The romantic myth says that if we have found the right person, the romance will last forever. The reality of life is that romance can never last forever, that the context and importance of romance changes across time, and that in every relationship there will exist hard times when it is not interesting, stimulating, and exciting to be together. In healthy, committed relationships, these are the times when we know we must once again work on ourselves. We must go inward to discover what we lack; we must spend whatever time it takes to fill our own needs and make our Selves happy or content. Looking externally, looking for the other to do something is trying to live the myth and is a part of our faulty training. If our partners let us be, now is the time to take advantage of their gift and to discover again who we are, what we want, and how to take care of our own needs.

Affairs

One of the most common reasons for separation occurs when one partner has been unfaithful to the other. Adultery always puts a strain on the marital relationship. There are many excuses given for looking outside the marriage: to feel good, to be understood and appreciated, to be sexually stimulated, to solve an unhappy situation, or to rediscover romantic love. Unfortunately none of these reasons for beginning an affair result in helping the marriage or even satisfying the straying partner. With few exceptions, and these usually involve untenable life situations, such as physical or mental illnesses that preclude the possibility of a normal sexual relationship within the marriage, most affairs are about trying to use external sources to resolve internal problems. Most adulterous relationships reflect insecurity and the avoidance of looking within to solve needs or wants. In this way they parallel other situations that we have experienced.

We may have decided to marry in order to stop feeling lonely, abandoned, or rejected, and we hoped our spouse would provide us with sexual satisfaction. We entered marriage thinking that our needs and wishes would be fulfilled. When this did not happen, because no one else can give us what we need, many of us turned to parenthood in order to find our life meaning. When we discovered that having children also did not fulfill us, we tried to seek what we were missing through our work. When our jobs did not completely satisfy our desires, then we may have considered or actually did turn to an outside relationship, an affair. It seems as if we will try anything to resolve our quest for unity, for belonging, for intimacy. Anything except working on our inner selves.

Pain Versus Gain

It is a very painful lesson to learn that what we so strongly crave can only be discovered by the journey within. Most of us would rather exhaust all external resources before we give up, give in, and go inside. Because this is such a common pattern, it must be that there is some merit in what is happening. Perhaps our developmental processes need exploration of all possibilities before we are ready to accept that what we are yearning for so desperately can only be found internally. We want the world to give us what we need; if our marriages, children, jobs, and friends cannot provide us with the answer to what is missing, then maybe a spicy, sexy, forbidden relationship will do so. At the very least it will provide a diversion from our painful search for meaning.

Affairs do not have to end in marital separation or divorce. They do not always mean the marriage is over, but they always do mean the marriage is changed. They can be used productively to help the marital relationship, as they clearly indicate what areas need change or work. The problem with using an affair to repair a marriage is that it usually hurts the couple's relationship so deeply that it requires an incredible amount of commitment, a lot of hard work, and a great deal of pain to resolve the marriage and relearn to trust. A good analogy here might be to think of the marriage as a leaky faucet, the affair as pulling out the pipes completely and flooding the room, and the therapist as the plumber. If we want the fix to be fast and cheap, the time to call for help is when it is leaking, before the affair.

Affairs Are Escape

Adultery is usually about excitement, control, some kind of communication (physical, emotional, sexual), and a return in some fashion to the glorious euphoria of falling in love. Even if love is not the primary motivater for this relationship, the very existence of this illicit joining provides a sense of excitement, drama, and release from the mundane, everyday world. Affairs take us out of time and place and put us into another dimension that can be highly addictive. Once again we feel really alive and we seem to have a purpose for being. What we have created is a double life, and stressful as it is, it fulfills our needs and consumes our energy. More than anything else, affairs release us from dwelling on our difficulties; they allow us to focus somewhere else, an exciting place that is simply more fun to be in. Mentally and physically they allow us to remove ourselves from the reality of our present lives, a reality that is lacking in something, or we would not be involved in the affair.

When we learn that this relationship, similar to all the others, cannot do for us what we really need and what we are looking for, we are left with more problems than we had before we tried to escape. We are facing a great deal of pain, some of it excruciating, for all concerned partners. Nobody gets away free and easy from this kind of involvement. While there may be lessons to be learned (there always is with pain), the cost may be very high. The irony here is that much of the pain caused by adultery is unnecessary and could have been avoided. We will stop seeking solutions in places where they cannot be found only when we each discover the reality of ourselves. Life demands that we live in reality in order to grow. Therefore anything that takes us out of reality, that presents a seductive escape from the resolution or working through our own problems, is dangerous and has the potential for great destruction and pain.

The Reality of Relationships

We cannot control when we are going to learn the important lessons that life will teach us. We cannot decide that it is time for us to discover something new just because we are tired of the old. When we have no choice in the matter, when it happens to us without any sense of control, then we are ready for the lesson. Healthy relationships give us the opportunity to keep on discovering ourselves. Often this ability occurs in the times that we do not feel wonderful about the relationship itself. There is a distinct difference between leaving an unhealthy relationship and staying in one that is essentially good but that is having a bad period. This difference can only be found by questioning the Self and being realistic about what the relationship can do for us. Relationships cannot give us self-love, self-worth, or self-esteem. This we must do for ourselves. They cannot provide the safety and security that we ourselves lack. However, they can nurture the development of such things within ourselves by providing an encouraging environment. Relationships are about challenge, growth, discovery, and mystery. They are the best arena in which we can practice our own spirituality and discover our souls and connections to the Whole.

When they cannot provide this arena, then separation and divorce are the alternatives. Taking this alternative, whether it is our choice or not, may be the best opportunity we ever encounter for discovering the Self. If it is true that no good deed ever goes unpunished, then perhaps it is also true that no painful (bad) deed that happens to us ever goes without some reward. If we view our separations as the opportunity for growth and the development of maturity and character, then we will be reframing current misery into future positive experience. We will be able to survive our present unhappiness and know that it will be the foundation for our future happiness. We will recognize that our feelings of being out of control will pave the way for our future feelings of stability and balance. We will be able to recognize the positive in what now feels so negative and hopeless. We will survive and we will emerge stronger, better, and more knowledgeable. We will take the gift of loss and go with it!

Finally, there is no better time to learn to love the Self than when we are feeling alone and unloved. This is the time to devote more energy to the Self, to take care of our own needs and wants, to be appreciative, loving, kind, nurturing, listening, caring, considerate—in fact all the things we hoped our partner would be but was not—to our Selves. If we can stop blaming the other or ourselves for the misery we are in and instead refocus on filling our own unfulfilled needs, we will be practicing self-esteem and Being. We will be assuming control over taking care of the Self and we will be generating love for the Self. This may be one of the most positive activities, with the greatest long-term results, that we will ever do in life. When we feel needy, fill the needs. When we feel unloved, practice being loving. When we feel lonely, practice Being, which is easier to do when we are alone. When we feel rejected, try acceptance. When we feel afraid, remember that courage is doing it anyway. When we feel a failure, recognize that surviving is everything. Learn that discipline is doing what we do not want to do. When we feel empty, give the Self rewards. And above all, during this difficult and hurting time, know that "This, too, shall pass." Nothing lasts forever, not even this pain. Thank God!

X ∞ Problem-Solving Separation and Divorce

1. Accepting

Accept that this is really happening to you. This may be one of your worst nightmares come true, but here it is and it is real. The relationship you have had, and may still badly want, is over. It simply does not work any longer, and one or both of you know that it must end. Accept that your present and future are now going to be very different from the way you previously hoped or imagined them to be, that, in a real way, everything has changed and life probably does not seem as safe, secure, or happy as it did before. At the very least it is no longer familiar and you are going to have to do things differently. Accept the hard fact that you may not get what you want and if you want this relationship to continue, you may be out of luck. Accept the fact that you are hurting and that it may well get worse before it gets better. Accept the reality of your situation *today* and not what it was yesterday.

You may feel abandoned, rejected, angry, sad, scared, helpless, hopeless, furious, repentant, justified, crazy, stoic, and calmly logical, almost all at the same time. You may bounce from feeling all right to wanting to die, and you may feel out of control one minute and perfectly in control the next. Accept that you are riding on an emotional roller coaster and that your feelings are not in your control. But most importantly accept yourself as you are and give yourself permission to be hurt, to feel whatever you feel, to grieve, to be needy, to be vulnerable; in short allow yourself to *be*. As painful as living in the present is, accept the fact that retreating to the past to escape your pain is futile and will only prolong the pain. Accept that the only way to get through the pain is to cope with it when it exists. This is not the time to deny your situation. Yes, you hurt horribly and will continue to hurt for a while, but eventually the pain will stop. This will not happen today and perhaps not tomorrow; accept that pain is now a reality of your life. You are changing, things are happening, and you will feel great again, but not yet. The degree to which you can benefit from your painful experience will depend upon your ability to accept and cope with the reality of it in the moment. You can do it, you are good, and you have great worth. Accept your situation so that you can begin the next step, letting go.

If you are still involved in the relationship, accept the reality of your present situation. Accept that you alone cannot change what is occurring and that you definitely cannot change your partner. If you truly believe that you have done everything you can to make things better but the relationship is still not working, accept that you do not have control and that the consequences are not your total responsibility. Accept that your relationship is a separate entity from either yourself or your partner; it exists with parts of each of you, but the relationship is not the totality of either of you. Perhaps you will need to accept that this relationship will not work for you and that its purpose, to teach you, has been accomplished and now you will need to move on.

2. Letting Go

This is one of your best opportunities to get rid of some of the myths and illusions about love that have brought you to the place you are now in. To begin with, let go of the idea that you have failed or are a failure. What have failed you are the unrealistic expectations about relationships that you have been taught. If you choose to continue to believe the myth of true love and to blame yourself for not living this illusion, then you must also realize that everyone else at some time or other has failed as well. Let go of the idea that you are the only one who cannot make a relationship work. Similarly let go of any idea that this is your fault and that you must therefore be unlovable. You are worthy of love, and this relationship is not the measure of your worth.

Let go of any desires to blame your partner for not reading your mind, not satisfying your desires, or for being responsible for what you are feeling. It may indeed be tempting to want to do so, and it may make you feel better in the short run to make your ex the reason for the end of the relationship. In some cases this may partly be true, but it will not help you to learn and grow if all your energy is spent on blame. Let go of any idea about revenge, for this will keep you involved, in a very destructive manner, in an unhealthy relationship with someone you now want to hurt more than you want to love. Let go of any obsessions about the other being the only one for you or the only person in the world whom you will love. This is not true, has never been true, and this is the worst time in your life to entertain such destructive fantasies. In the same way let go of idealizing or glamorizing the relationship you had. This relationship is now over, it is gone, it belongs in the past, and it did not work.

Let go of recriminations, regrets, and remorse. Let go of any thoughts that punish you at this time. You are vulnerable and in pain and this is not the time for self-flagellation. Let go of trying to think in terms of "What if's" or "If only's," for these are not realistic and will only serve to prolong your pain. At times you may even need to try to let go of making complete sense or wholly understanding all facets of what has happened. You will never be able to get into your partner's head, heart, or body. You never could when you were with your partner and you cannot do so now. Trying to mind-read, second-guess, or make sense out of every word, thought, or action will only make you feel crazy.

You have already changed, your partner has also changed, the relationship has changed; trying to dissect something that is no longer there is another exercise in futility. It may be very difficult to admit to yourself that you do not have all the answers, all the reasons, all the comprehension about what went wrong in your relationship. Let go of your need to know, understand, and make sense of all of it. Work on your part of it; focus on what you did, how you felt, what did not work for you. This is the part of the relationship that will teach you what you need to know. This is the only part that will eventually make sense for you. By letting go of what you cannot control and instead focusing on what you can, you will be constructively learning about yourself in relationships. You will be actively setting the foundation for your future ones, the ones that will work for you.

3. Expressing Feelings

You already recognize that your emotions seem to be all over the place. You may never before have felt so many different feelings in such close proximity. You may feel like a rubber ball, bouncing off all the walls, because your mood shifts are so rapid, unexpected, and not in your control. This is one of those times in life when it is absolutely normal to be a quivering mass of feelings. When you are in emotional pain, as with physical pain, the first thing that occurs is shock, which serves as an anesthetic to buffer the beginnings of great pain. This quickly wears off, leaving unbelievable pain. This is usually not constant, but waxes and wanes, growing and diminishing in intensity. You may feel that it is ever present, but if you attend to your pain, you will see that at times it is much worse and at other times it is more manageable. As you get better, you will observe that the frequency of manageable times increases. Each day will bring some lessening of the pain and a growing comfort as what is happening to you becomes familiar.

Recognize that you are emotionally unstable and that this will affect all areas of your life. You cannot separate yourself from your feelings and continue as if nothing has happened to you. If you try to do so, you risk being cut off from your feelings and becoming emotionally disconnected from life. You are no longer what you were before; you are in the process of life change, and your pain is the catalyst for what you are becoming. Be easy on yourself; do not expect your functioning to be what it was when you were not hurting. You have probably not been taught how to handle emotional pain effectively. Most of us have been raised to try to be strong and stoic in the midst of it. If you were hurting physically as much as you are currently aching emotionally, how would you treat yourself? You would certainly not expect to be as strong, confident, clear-headed, and capable as you were before. You will be those things again, but you are not them today. Know that this is normal: You get to hurt, you are supposed to hurt, it is appropriate to hurt in your situation.

This is an excellent time to express your feelings, all your feelings, when you are alone, with a therapist, or with a trusted friend. While it is true that you cannot control what you are feeling, remember that you can control how you are behaving and what you choose to do with your emotions. Falling apart at work or in inappropriate places is not going to help you get over your grief. You may need to take breaks, take extra time off, be restrictive of your activities so that you can have some control over your behavior. If you allow yourself to fall apart when you are at home or in safe places, you can often keep yourself together when you have to. Try to structure your time in such a way that you have time to yourself every day. Practice letting your feelings come out in your time and place; in this way you will be able to assert more control over yourself. When you are physically ill, you take time off to get well. Do the same here—take mental health time for yourself.

Because so many of your feelings are directed at or about your partner, who is probably no longer available to receive them, write letters that you will never send to your ex. Do not censor what you are feeling as you write; allow the anger, the hatred, the negativity to spew out of you onto the written page. You are getting these feelings, which do exist, out of you and you are getting rid of them. This will eventually feel liberating and cleansing. You do not want to carry all this negativity around with you any longer. Also write all the things you regret or wish you had known and done differently. It is too late to go back and do them, so write them in order to get free from them. This is usually an excellent time to seek professional help in order to move from the destructive to the constructive work that needs to be done. You are grieving, you are in pain, you are changing, and you may well need help to get you back on track. Support groups and close friends can be invaluable for you. Try to find as many resources as you can to help you through the pain; the more resources available to you, the less chance you will overextend any single one. You do not want to become a burden to someone you care about just because you are burdened with grief.

4. Taking Responsibility

Please do not begin this step until you have completed the previous ones. Usually you will be tempted to do one of two things when a close relationship ends: (a) blame the other for everything; or (b) blame yourself. Playing the blame game seems to stop the pain for a while; after all, it is easier to feel anger than it is to feel sadness. Anger gives you an illusion of strength and control. When you are angry, you feel energized and righteous. Feeling sad, on the other hand, tends to diminish any illusions of control. Therefore sadness is the more difficult, but more realistic feeling. Blaming is about anger; accepting is admitting the sadness that exists.

Taking responsibility for your part in what has happened to your relationship is not something you can do immediately or quickly. It involves a learning process and an awareness of the changes that have happened to you. Oftentimes you cannot see what you are doing when you are involved in relating, but you need the objectivity provided by time and distance in order to perceive your role in the relationship accurately. Now that it is over, you are no longer what you were when it was ongoing. What you see and understand at this time may have been impossible back then. You cannot go back with your new perceptions and understandings and fix the past. You can only take your new awareness with you into the future by using it in the present.

Once again, only take responsibility for what was in your control at that time. Take the onus for these actions onto yourself and then let go of them. You are learning as soon as you are aware of your part; you do not have to carry this responsibility for what you once did with you for the rest of your life. What you will learn from this is that you are responsible for your life, your behavior, and what is in your control, and you can utilize this knowledge and awareness productively now and in the future. In other words let go of your mistakes, your wrongdoings, your failures after you have recognized and realistically accepted that these were yours. You will never be perfect and your relationships will never be perfect. However, you can learn from your mistakes—that is the purpose of recognizing them. Let them teach you what you need to know and then let them go. Be as sorry as you need to be, to yourself and to the ones you have hurt. Learn from this also and let it go. The worse the mistake, the greater the lesson and the less likely you will be to repeat it. When something really hurts, you will remember the effects of the pain long after you have forgotten the pain itself. So it is with errors. Beating yourself up for the past is dumb. As a matter of fact beating yourself up for anything is self-destructive and a waste of learning time. Face up to your faults, accept your mistakes, take responsibility for what is yours, make amends when you can, and learn to do it differently next time. This is the secret of always being the best that you can be, for yourself.

5. Forgiving

Begin this step by forgiving yourself for all the things above for which you have taken responsibility. Go through all your mistakes, all the things you wish you had not said or done, all your past errors and forgive yourself. This may sound quite simple, but in reality this is a very difficult task to do well. You have been taught to justify, explain, defend, deny, and rationalize your misdeeds. In order to forgive yourself for them, you must first take the responsibility and this goes against your training. If you do manage to complete this step fully and completely and you can forgive yourself for your part in what happened to the relationship, you may indeed feel overwhelmed by your own shortcomings and failures, your lack of awareness and sensitivity. Remember to forgive yourself for not knowing, for not being perfect. This step, the ability to forgive yourself, is a critical one to begin before you become lost in recriminations.

Forgiving yourself for your part in the separation or divorce may seem too difficult to do well. You might have the tendency to do this superficially, by giving yourself a blanket forgiveness for everything. This will not result in the cleansing and the awareness that you will need to change and begin again. Listing the specific actions that you did, remembering the things that you probably feel embarrassed or ashamed about, and being realistic and objective as you take inventory of your failings is a lot of work and cannot be done effectively if you try to rush past this stage. Forgiving yourself really means letting go of your insecurities, unfulfilled and unrealistic illusions, and some of your dreams. It means facing yourself fully and completely and taking a good, long, hard look at who you are, what you have done, and what you most need. When you can really see all this, then absolve yourself, understanding that you are truly human—flawed and imperfect—but you are struggling to learn.

You are doing a heroic task and you deserve forgiveness for not always knowing how to do it right. You have hurt others, you have hurt yourself needlessly, and you will never exist without inflicting some pain. When you can accept this, and forgive yourself, a paradox occurs: Recognizing that you cause pain means that you will cause less pain. Forgiving yourself for being human means that paradoxically you will be rising above your human condition. Absolution, first of self and then of others, is the beginning of true spirituality, the recognition that goodness prevails.

Now that you have truly forgiven yourself, forgive your partner for his (or her) part in the relationship difficulties. Once you have forgiven yourself, you have done the hard part. Forgiving others is usually easier. Do not carry around any unnecessary pain and negativity. Forgive them, especially if they are not able to forgive themselves or be objective about what has happened. Remember, you cannot change anyone else, but you can let them go. Forgiveness means you have truly let the other person go and you can now allow them to be, separate from yourself.

6. Appreciating

This is a step that cannot occur early on in the separation process. This step only occurs after the completion of the preceding steps. Once you start coming out of your pain, once you clearly see that you will be all right, that life holds new promises and that what has happened to you has relevance and meaning, then you can begin to appreciate what you have learned. You will discover that there are many things to appreciate about the experience you have gone through. You will begin to see that your past relationships and your breakup have taught you many valuable lessons, not the least of which is an expanded awareness of who you are and what you want. When you are ready to recognize that what has happened to you has been a valuable, albeit painful, learning experience, then you are ready to appreciate the lessons you have learned.

Please don't forget to appreciate yourself in this process. Give thanks that you have survived, you have come through the terrible pain, you have risen above your worst fears and insecurities. You have become stronger, wiser, more empathetic, and less judgmental of others. Because you have been so miserable, you can relate to the misery of others. Because you have had moments of deep despair and irrational thinking, you can relate to others when they are demonstrating the same feelings or thoughts. Because you now know how very little control you have had, you can be more tolerant of others who are unable to control their lives. If this was your first time to be deeply hurt, recognize that you have survived the bottom of the well and you no longer have to fear it. You no longer have to be afraid of what you know and have overcome. You have done a heroic job getting to this place; appreciate your efforts and your survival. You deserve it!

After you have appreciated your own efforts and achievements, then you can appreciate what your partner has given you. This relationship has given you more opportunity for change and growth, learning and development, and it has done this relatively rapidly in the scheme of time, than any of your less emotional and perhaps more successful relationships. Success is never the teacher that failure can be. What has not worked for you in the ways in which you imagined has now worked for you in ways you never dreamed of. You have been significantly altered, your life has changed, and you have become aware of the emotional highs and depths that you possess. Your ex has provided the opportunity for this to occur. Appreciate this fact, even if you cannot completely appreciate the person. If you can appreciate that your old partner is also struggling to learn and grow, you will be giving yourself a wonderful gift. You can only appreciate after you have truly let go and forgiven; this step is a true test of your maturity and understanding of what it means to be human.

7. Rewarding

Now is the time to learn to reward yourself. After all, you have been through one of the most difficult times in your life and you have survived. Reward yourself generously. Give your Self exactly what you need. Be kind to you. If you had placed all your worth and esteem with others, especially your partner, you have now learned to esteem yourself. This deserves a big reward because you have learned one of the most painful lessons in life. No one else can love you exactly the way you most want to be loved, but you can love yourself this way. Loving yourself is in itself a reward, but it is a task that requires encouragement along the way. Self-love is process; it is re-enforced by giving yourself what you most need and want. Say the kinds of things you say to others when they have succeeded in getting through a difficult time—now say them to yourself. Reward yourself by being kind, generous, loving, considerate, and concerned—to you.

Reward yourself for the recognition that no relationship with another is necessary for making you whole or balanced. You are complete and you are okay all by yourself. You have probably learned that loneliness and aloneness are not the same thing. Reward yourself for this awareness. Give yourself something nice every day. Buy yourself a small gift, bake something you love just for you, pay yourself a wonderful compliment, smile at yourself in the mirror, tell yourself that you are wonderful and that you are worthy of the very best in life. By rewarding yourself you will be reinforcing what you have done to survive the pain and you will not take yourself for granted for achieving what you have. Good relationships are about kindness, respect, and appreciation. When you reward yourself, you are actively demonstrating these skills. You have done a great job. You get to be rewarded for your efforts. Never again do you have to wait for external recognition; now you have learned how to recognize yourself. This is a major achievement. Go for it!

XI ↝ *Friends*

Of all our relationships with others, friendships may be the most important, and in many ways the least complicated. To varying degrees we are all social animals, and the majority of our social life concerns our friendships. We can do quite well as adults without close family relationships; we can exist quite well (some may say very well) without significant love relationships. Some of us choose not to have spouses or children; but we all need at least one good friend. A friend can be defined as someone we can share with, someone to talk to and to listen to, whose opinion we value, who is there for us, and for whom we can be there. Most importantly a friend is someone we can laugh with and another pair of eyes looking at this crazy world and sharing perceptions with us. A friend therefore enriches us, enhances us, expands our perceptions, and helps us to make sense of what we see. How, then, can friends become a problem?

Types of Problems

One difficulty with friends is quantitative: too few versus too many of them. It may be easy to understand how not having any can be a huge problem—we have all had times when we yearned for one or two close friends to share our experiences and ease our loneliness. It may be more difficult to conceive how too many friends, or too much friendship time, can be a problem. As with most things, there must be a balance. In this case it is between time alone and time with others. Not having time with others, not having friends, clearly throws life off balance. Too much solitude, as with too much of anything else, becomes a problem, since time alone can easily become lonely time. The opposite is also a problem: Too much friendship time can also throw life out of balance. Constant input from others can lead to escapism from ourselves. We may begin to value being with our friends so much that we forget the value of being alone. If we spend all available time with friends, we may easily slip into the pattern of needing external stimulation in order to feel alive. In other words we may find our own company boring and we may create an unhealthy need for others in order to keep ourselves entertained. This is clearly true during preadolescence, when friendships are intense and all-consuming. Then this style is developmentally appropriate; later on it is not.

As is true of all our relationships, those with friends can easily become problems when we become dependent, too needy, and overattached. If we think back over our history with friends, we may indeed see a pattern. When we have a history of frustrating relationships, of many friends for a short period of time, but few, if any, for the long term, we probably have a dependent style with them. As children we are critically needy of friends in order to feel safe, accepted, and important. Many children create invisible friends to help satisfy their needs and allay their fears. Again these actions are indicative of the developmental process. As adults we cannot seek to satisfy our needs through others, unless we are developmentally delayed.

The Beauty of Friendship

Unlike the other relationships that have been discussed, friendship is usually not about commitment. We may eventually become committed to our friend, but we do not begin the relationship with the idea of long-term goals. We usually start by letting the other person be whoever he is and by sharing thoughts and feelings, with little or no expectations of agreement. In other words we are somewhat interested in what he (or she) thinks or feels, but if he does not agree with us, that is usually fine. We like some commonality, but we do not expect or demand it. Therein lies the beauty of friendship: You are and I am and we have nothing to prove or disprove. I am being and you are being and we are both accepting of the other. If not, we do not become friends. If so, we do, and we share more and spend more time together. If I begin our relationship by not being what I am, but by being what I think you want me to be, I am not developing a friendship. I am creating a coercive relationship. I am acting a part that, in some form, you will have to pay for. I am setting you up, not to be my friend but to be something more, perhaps my savior, martyr, or codependent.

Real friendships are based on the premise that we will enrich and enhance each other by allowing each of us to be ourself. Good friendships are all about acceptance and letting go. They are about balance. If I am needy in some capacity, then you also get to be needy. If I am strong at times, then you, too, get to be strong at other times. If I can give to you, then you also get to give to me. When we disagree, it is a matter of interest and not the end of the world. And when we both agree, we congratulate each other on having such a smart friend. Friendships are about fun and learning to laugh at ourselves and with others. When we cannot do the above, then the friendship is in the problem stage.

Importance of Boundaries

Another definition, and an important distinction between parents, spouses, and children is that a friend is someone who does *not* live with us. The boundaries for friends are clearly defined by the space inherent in not living under the same roof. When we do live all the time with another, our relationship fundamentally changes. Often it does not change for the better. Some of us may have had the experience of a friend who later became our roommate. For some this circumstance may have deepened the relationship, but not without a lot of work and compromise and open communication. For others, living together caused the friendship to deteriorate. If we could not accept that the relationship had fundamentally changed, it most likely fell apart. This is because the friend relationship we once had is no longer as simple once we share the same home. The types of problems that we have seen in our original and chosen families and with lovers tend to surface when two people spend long periods of time under the same roof. Therefore it becomes easy to recognize the significant distinction between a good friend and a spouse or someone that we live with: The friend can be there for us at times, but then gets to leave; a live-in relationship, be it spouse or roommate, does not get to leave (at least not as easily or painlessly). A friend is someone who can come and go in our lives and who is not sharing multiple facets of our lives. There are good, healthy friendships in which the people live together, even work together, but these extend past the normal relationship boundaries of friendship into family situations. We may call our spouse our best friend, but we can recognize that this relationship also extends the boundaries of normal friendships. These time and space boundaries are important because they automatically provide the separation that is necessary for a healthy friendship.

Healthy Versus Unhealthy Friendships

The key words in defining relationship problems with friends have already been mentioned: neediness (dependency), unrealistic expectations, need for commitment, boredom, loneliness, not being real, and being out of balance. When our friendships are not working, one or more of these is probably occurring. Perhaps a good rule here is: Friends are there for us, but they are not there to take care of us. It then follows that we are there for our friends, but we also are not there to take care of them. If we look at these concepts, we can see that this is not the way that we have been brought up to think about relationships. Most of us have been taught that we are supposed to take care of others, especially those we care about. Many of us have probably been in friendships where we have been overextended and too much has been expected from us. These are about codependency in the same ways that our family and love relationships are.

When friends are demanding too much from us, or when we demand too much from them, there is a problem. Demands are another form of unrealistic expectations. However, a lack of any requests of the relationship may also reflect unrealistic (and unrealized) expectations. What this means is that there must be some balance between what we give and what we take. We can have some realistic expectations for our friends: We can ask them to be reasonably loyal to us, to be supportive at times, and to value our friendship as much as we value theirs. We can expect them to avoid deliberately trying to hurt us, while understanding that they may do so inadvertently. We cannot expect them to be able to read our minds or always to know what we want and need, even when we do not. We cannot expect them always to need us, but instead we recognize that it is healthy for them to be able to take care of themselves.

However, this does not mean they do so by always putting themselves above us or using us. Taking care of their own needs and wants is healthy; putting them onto us to take care of is not. We do not need friends who are constant work for us, just as we do not want them to feel that their relationship with us is a burden. We do not want friends who are constantly critical of everything we do or say. On the other hand we do not need them to agree with every word we utter. Neither tyrants nor clones are true or healthy friends. The best friends we can have are those who know themselves, who are secure in themselves and can be supportive of us, and, most important of all, who let us be. In order to have friends who meet these descriptions, we will need to be the same. Our friends can model these traits for us, but they cannot make us secure in ourselves. They cannot do our life work, but they surely can encourage the doing of it and they can provide comfort, companionship, and lots of laughter along the way.

Friends as Role Models

We can have many different kinds of friendships and each one can bring out a different facet of ourselves. Our friends can serve a variety of roles for us and can function to expand our repertoires and enhance our lives. The roles that friends provide can effortlessly change across time and situation. Old, well-known friends can give us a sense of security and safety in a world that does not often provide us with these attributes. New friends can provide stimulation, interest, and excitement. Through them we can perceive that we ourselves are not constant, that our roles and interests change with different people. We can have a sense of our maturation, growth, and development. Thus friends can teach us that life is ever changing, and so are we. They can provide us with new arenas in which to experiment and new ways in which to perceive life. Perhaps the best thing friends do for us is their modeling of different facets of life and behavior. When we have a wide variety of friends of different ages and backgrounds, we are provided with a vast repertoire of options. Our friends help us to increase our choices, expand our possibilities, and grow internally.

Therefore friendships function in a very different manner from family relationships or intimate love relationships. For one thing we can be more realistic about our expectations and we can recognize that we do not ask one friend to be all things to us. We are usually less invested in what they can do and who they are. We know some friends are for fun while others are for more serious times. We trust different ones in different ways. We see the faults and the strengths of our friends with more objective and often more loving eyes than we do with those we live with. It is easier to let our friends *be,* and we can learn from this to let ourselves and our intimates also *be.*

The Advantage of Friendships

Because friends are so important in our lives, problems with them can be emotionally devastating and time-consuming. The one advantage here is that unless we have allowed our problematic friendship to become the center of our lives, we will have other areas of our lives to retreat to when our friendship is in trouble. We will have family, or beloveds, or other friends to help us through the difficulty. Most friendship relationships do not involve the degree of commitment or the intensity that causes us the great pain when the relationship is over. It is easier to change our expectations and illusions about our friends than it is to change those about our family or lovers. We can continue a friendship that has been changed, whereas it is often impossible to do so with a lover. Because we expect less from friends than we usually do from family, it is easier to make allowances for friends. Usually we want our friends to do what they need to do in their lives; this is not as simple with those with whom our lives are entwined. We generally do not depend on one individual friend to fill all our friendship needs; we spread the wealth around. This is different with our families and significant others, as they tend to carry a higher burden and pay a bigger price for their relationship with us.

We can learn a great deal from friends: We can practice being friendly to ourselves and our families. What we do with our friends we can also do with our Self. We can begin by letting *be*. We can lower our expectations and raise our encouragement. We can demand less and accept more. We can recognize that boundaries exist between us and others, and we can respect and appreciate them. How we behave with friends is how we can learn to behave with everyone. We can learn to expect and even welcome change and we can recognize the other's ability to take care of his or her own needs. We can be there when necessary, because we want to, and we can relinquish our needs to be needed. We can recognize that we deserve to be treated well, just as others deserve the same. Friends can be marvelous teachers; friendship lessons are those that can be extended and applied to all our relationships.

XII ⌒ Problem-Solving Friends

1. Accepting

If you are having a problem with a friend, accept the fact that this difficulty exists. Do not waste time imagining how it could be different. Deal with the fact that something is wrong, something is not working for you, and that you are uncomfortable or unhappy. Recognize that you are not perfect, your friend is not perfect, and no relationship can ever be perfect. In addition things happen that you do not expect or like. Remember, you cannot control your friends or their lives and they cannot control you. When you can accept how very little control you do have, then you can also accept how little control your friends have. Recognize that there is always another side to the situation and that your friend may have a different perspective. Try to be objective rather than emotional in evaluating what is wrong. Accepting the reality of your situation is always the beginning of problem solving. You do not have to act on anything at this point. Acceptance does not mean change. It is about what is rather than what could be. Whatever you are feeling, accept. Your feelings will not end or change anything, but your behaviors might. In this stage you are not deciding what to do, but you are recognizing clearly what is happening.

2. Letting Go

In any problem with a friend let go of your concept of what each of you *should* be doing. As a matter of fact let go of the concept of "should." Forget the idea that either of you knows what is best for the other. Let go of righteous indignation and codependency (doing for the other what he or she is not willing or able to do for himself). Do not get caught up in who or what is right and who or what is wrong. Remember that two rights can often lead to wrong and two wrongs never lead to right. You may know that you are right, but if your friend does not agree, what good is it? Let go of the idea that because your friend knows you, he can read your mind or know what you need or want. Forget your fantasies of what a perfect friendship is about and that all your friends must measure up to your standards, or that you must measure up to theirs. Also let go of unrealistic expectations about your friends or what their relationships with you can do for you. Friendships, as is true of all relationships, cannot in and of themselves make you happy, secure, or give you self-esteem. Stop trying to make them do so. Friendships are about enhancing your life, not about giving you a life. Friends are similar to the rewards of life—they are the icing on your existence. They cannot make the cake for you; only you can do that.

3. Expressing Feelings

Express your feelings about your problem or difficulty with your friend as clearly and as openly as possible. One definition of friendship is a relationship in which you can express your feelings honestly. Intimacy depends upon sharing feelings in a safe environment. Expressing them is quite different from placing blame. Your feelings are yours. Own them. Tell your friend what you are feeling without placing the responsibility for your feeling onto him. For example, saying "I am hurt" has quite a different effect on the listener than "You are hurting me." Remember to allow your friend also to express his feelings.

If you cannot express your feelings directly to your friend, for whatever reason, at the very least express them to yourself. Get those feelings out. Do not worry about justifying or rationalizing them at this point. The fact that you have them is justification enough for expressing them. Sometimes the act of expression is enough for the feelings to move on. Sometimes you will be angry or hurt or frustrated and will know, at a cognitive level, that it is not the other person's fault. In these cases it is best to express your feelings to yourself, or to a neutral person. If you are overly emotional or out of control, it is probably wise to get your feelings out when you are alone. In these situations it helps to rehearse what you want to say so that you can be clear and clean when you do confront your friend. If you are in a rage, beat up your own pillow. If your pain is causing incoherence and a deluge of tears, cry and yell and use up your own box of tissues before you deal with your friend. When you are calm and in control and able to communicate, then you can deal with letting the other person know how you are feeling.

Your emotional state can never be an excuse to beat up on another, be it friend, foe, or whomever. Your emotional condition is you, and no one else can be held accountable for your feelings. Yes, your friend has hurt you or done something, and now you are upset. But this is your pain and your anger. Just as you owe it to yourself not to let others deliberately abuse or misuse you, so you also do not have the right to inflict unnecessary pain (that which can be avoided) on others. You simply do not have the right to victimize others because you are upset. Your pillow can be the victim for your anger; your tissues can fall victim to your tears. Your friends are not objects to be used but are individuals who need to be treated with dignity and respect, just as you expect to be treated that way by them.

4. Taking Responsibility

In all relationships, including those with your friends, it is important to be honest about what is your fault, what is your responsibility, and what is in your control. Remember, you cannot be responsible for something over which you do not have control. Conversely you are responsible for what you do control. You have complete control over what you choose to feel about yourself (self-esteem means choosing to feel good about yourself) and how you behave. You also have responsibility over your choices, including your choice of friends. These friends are not responsible for what you feel or how you behave. They cannot live your life, make your decisions, or make you feel good or bad. You are making a choice, you are responsible for your behavior, when you react to them. In other words your actions are in your control, and reacting is your choice of behavior. You are empowering them (in a negative way) when you blame them for your feelings or your behavior. Take control of yourself. Nobody can make you feel bad or behave inappropriately unless you let him. Nobody is more powerful than you are, unless you give him your personal power.

It may well be true that your friends exert powerful influences over you. You may be in need of more than your friends can give when you allow them to rule your life, make your decisions, or determine your emotional state. You may be involved in a destructive trade-off: abdicating personal autonomy in order to get the feeling of belonging with others. If so, you are probably reliving a pattern from your childhood that you have not sufficiently worked through. The beginning of all life resolutions occurs when you assume responsibility. Once you do this, you begin bringing your life under your own control, where it belongs. Anyone who resists this process or who is opposed to your gaining independence is not your friend.

5. Forgiving

Forgive your friends for making mistakes, for not being perfect, for being human. Forgive yourself the same. Even if you decide that you no longer desire them to be your trusted, close friends, pardon them as you let them go. Forgiveness is important for allowing others to be. Friendships are based on allowing others to be what they are. Forgive your friends for not being what you may want and absolve yourself from not being what they may want.

Forgiveness is not condescension. It is not about judging and looking down on others from some better, higher perch. It is about understanding other people and why they are doing what they are doing. It involves putting yourself in their position, viewing the world through their eyes, and then letting go and letting be. Forgiveness involves empathy and caring and some degree of objectivity. It is the opposite of carrying a grudge or seeking revenge. The problem of paybacks or getting even or trying to impose fairness upon life is that these things place you in the position of enacting the same type of behavior that created the problem for you. It is impossible to feel that you are being the best you can be when you are engaging in actions that cause pain and that you yourself do not like when they are being done to you. It is very difficult to love yourself when you are doing things you do not like. Forgiveness is the way out of this negative loop.

6. Appreciating

Appreciate the opportunities your friends have given you. Your problems with them can be reframed as challenges for your growth and learning. Your difficulties with friends have helped you to develop your value system and principles. When others did things you did not like or approve of, their actions helped you understand how you perceive your world and what is important for you. Your friends have taught you many things. They have given you different ways of seeing and understanding this crazy world. They have supported you, shared themselves with you, laughed and cried and dreamed with you. Your life has more meaning and value because of their being. Tell them so. Appreciate their contributions to your education, and when it has been painful or imperfect, appreciate it even more. Share with them your thankfulness. And then do not forget to appreciate your enrichment of your friends' lives. You have been a good friend, you have cared and shared, gone out of your way, questioned yourself before you questioned them, tried to help in the best way you know how. Appreciate all of this, especially when your friends do not.

7. Rewarding

Reward your friends for being valuable to you. Tell them how much you appreciate them. Share with them what they have taught you and how they have helped you. Reward them with your time, your interest, and your attention. Reward them by being there for them when you can. Reward them and yourself by having fun. Play together, laugh together, and cry together. All of this is rewarding. Sharing yourself is the highest compliment you can give to another. Really being with someone else enhances life. Reward the friends you love and trust by being what you really are—be yourself around them. Reward them by dropping the facade and by being real. When you can do this, you will discover that you are rewarding, your friends are rewarding, and life itself becomes rewarding. The more rewards you give, the more you will receive. When your life is filled with good friends, feelings of accomplishment and caring, then you will be truly living the "rewarding life."

Let us work without disputing;
it is the only way to render life tolerable.

—Voltaire

XIII ⌒ *Colleagues and Co-workers*

People who we work with can and often do become our friends, but not everyone with whom we spend time in the work setting is a friend. Usually most of the people we work with are considered colleagues or co-workers rather than friends. And we have different kinds of relationships with them. The main reason for having and continuing this kind of association is the work; these relationships are initiated by and limited to our work and its environment. Because we spend a large part of our time with the people we work around, it is natural that we will get to know some of them quite well. The criteria for becoming friends are knowing each other, spending time together, and sharing some of the same interests. All of these things happen with our co-workers, but relatively few of them become our friends. This is usually because the work setting is the only shared focus and we do not get to choose the people with whom we work.

Importance of Choice

Choice is a critical distinction between friends and co-workers. Because our choice in this environment is restricted or nonexistent, colleagues we do not like can become some of our biggest relationship problems. Usually if we do not like people, we simply decide not to be around them. In the workplace we do not have the luxury of this choice. Our lives can be made miserable by having to be near someone who "drives us crazy" or who "gets on our nerves." There is nothing more frustrating than having to deal with someone who picks on us, makes us constantly upset, is unsupportive or uncaring, and who has different values from ours. Most of us have experienced such a situation with a co-worker. When this happens, we may find that we are becoming obsessed and that our quality of life has diminished due to this negative work relationship. We may even find that we are becoming less than what we want to be as a result of trying to retaliate or defend ourselves against our adversarial co-worker. We may not know how to deal with the harassment, emotional abuse, or stubbornness. In the worst case we may even discover that the other parts of our lives are being affected by this destructive relationship.

Power Problems

There are many reasons for difficulties in the workplace. One of the critical problems that frequently occurs is the issue of power and control. This makes sense when we consider our training and our needs to be perceived as successful. We have been taught that we are what we *do* and for most of us this translates into finding ourselves through our jobs or careers. Therefore being successful means being powerful, being paid well, and being seen by others as having control, importance, and recognition; the work arena becomes the critical environment in which to prove ourselves. This leads to competition with co-workers, a need to be in charge, to be respected, and to be consistently promoted in order to be successful. These expectations about our needs and desires do not make for healthy, cohesive, collegial relationships, but rather tend to separate people and cause mistrust and negative or destructive behavior.

These problems are compounded when there is very little real power to be distributed in the environment, leaving co-workers to compete over illusory power. We all need our moments of power, of feeling we have some control. The most difficult problems occur when there is very little actual power and everybody is fighting for his or her piece of the pie. Nothing can create as much disharmony and negativity in the work environment as this issue. Smart, intelligent, sweet people can turn into back-stabbing, competitive, unreasonable, and difficult co-workers when they are denied their illusion of power and control. When we confuse our success in life with our success at work, we are vulnerable to (and we propagate) the disharmonious, discouraging work setting.

The Myth of the Western Model

A related factor in this difficult work environment is the issue of responsibility without control. The negative work arena is one in which responsibility is given to many, but control is held by few. In other words we are held responsible for things we cannot control. This is a similar pattern to that in which a child feels responsible for his or her parents, who have the control. In this case the worker takes on what rightfully belongs to a superior. If the boss delegates responsibility, but retains the power, then the worker is going to be in a no-win situation. Many of us get stuck in such dilemmas and perpetuate them due to our need to be perceived by others as responsible or capable of doing whatever it takes to get the job done. After all, isn't this part of our training, part of the myth of being successful? We are taught that we have to do whatever is necessary; we learn that perseverance and determination will allow us to do the impossible. This myth is powerful, and the illusion defining success is stronger than the reality that we cannot do everything and we cannot be perfect. We believe the myth because it is part of our familiar American work ethic: We can do, we will win. We glamorize our success stories and ignore the reality behind many of our work heroes—the workaholic disorder. The price of success can be too high, the cost of climbing the ladder can destroy our balance, self-esteem, creativity, and best qualities.

Following the Doing model for success can cause us to forget the rest of our lives and become out of balance. The conflict here is that it is a highly addictive model and one that our society reinforces very strongly. Even when we discover this is not what we want, most of our colleagues and co-workers will still be following it. The work environment will not easily or quickly change; competition and the need to win will remain the desired tenets for most of society. We may choose to give up the rat race, but the work environment will still reflect others' needs to succeed, to climb to the top, to be the biggest and the best. By electing to reprioritize our values, become more balanced, get out of the craziness, we will be setting ourselves up to be viewed as different. We may even be considered as not part of the team and no longer a key player. This can lead to even more problems for us, due to our inherent needs to belong, to be united, to work together, and to work in harmony. There may be no easy solution to this dilemma, but the only answer is to remain true to the Self.

Personality Problems

Another issue that causes great dissension in the workplace is that we will at some time have to deal with difficult people. There will always be somebody who is creating problems for us. This may be somebody who simply does not like us or whom we do not like, or it can be an individual with personality problems or emotional disorders that make it impossible to get along with them. Unfortunately, while it is usually easy to recognize those with physical or mental conditions, it can be very difficult to recognize personality and emotional disorders. Paranoid personalities; sociopaths; passive-aggressive, dependent, borderline, and narcissistic people are often highly intelligent, competent, capable, and crafty. Many of these personality disorders manifest themselves through skilled manipulations; these are people who have spent their entire lives knowing how to work others in order to get their own needs met. One important reality here is that these problematic ones simply do not think and feel in a normal way. When we are reasonably emotionally healthy, our tendency is to believe that others think, act, and respond in ways similar to ours. Therefore we tend to project our own feelings and actions onto others. Generally we try to think in terms of what we would do in that situation. We will also find excuses or rationalizations for behavior when it does not fit our projection. When we do so, we become vulnerable for assuming or taking responsibility for such people.

People with personality disorders are by definition difficult people who cause problems. Being aligned with them will create a great deal of unnecessary work and in the end little recognition or reward. Being against them will fuel their disorder; they thrive on dissension and are quite skilled at drawing up battle lines and marshaling forces to help them fight. If the workplace feels like a war zone, chances are there are personality-disordered co-workers operating. One reason for a warlike environment is that emotionally disturbed individuals tend to have chaotic internal states, which only feel comfortable and familiar when the external environment is also chaotic. Therefore they will create tension and thrive in it. When everyone else is uncomfortable and insecure, they will look strong, comfortable, and powerful. When things are going well and harmony prevails, they become upset and unsure.

Personality disorders are quite common; therefore there is an excellent chance that most of us will have some experience with people who have them. These emotionally dysfunctional individuals will present a great challenge for us to overcome. The problems we will face with them will not be small or insignificant, as they will cause us to examine ourselves, our motivations, feelings, needs, and dark sides in ways that our friends never will. We may perceive ourselves as kind and considerate, just and reasonable, caring and sane, until we become either the good friend or the bad enemy of the co-worker with a personality disorder. Then we will encounter problems that waste time, work that seems unnecessary, and experiences that cause us to question how much we can give, how much we can tolerate, and finally how much we will rebel.

The Challenge

There are two simple questions we can ask if we think we are caught up in such a sticky situation: (a) how much self-esteem this colleague has versus how much weak ego—is he able to give himself what he needs or is he constantly looking to others to fill his needs for worth? (b) Is he able to take responsibility for his own feelings and actions, or is he always blaming them on something external? When we ask these questions of ourselves, we get a measure of our own esteem and idependence. When we ask them of our problematic colleagues, we also get a measure of their disorder. The criteria for a healthy personality are found in the answers to these questions. Our balance and strength exist in our own independence and in our ability to take care of ourselves and to take responsibility for what we do and who we are. Personality disorders exist in those who are unable to know themselves, lack a sense of identity, and are unable to take responsibility for themselves, and their behavior.

Remember, we do not live in a vacuum. In order to feel good about ourselves, we do need support and encouragement from others. Negative relationships are by their very nature discouraging and destructive. We can learn from them, but in the work environment this learning process can be very expensive. Unlike friendships, which we can leave without financial consequences, a work relationship is tied in to our job security, livelihood, and professional success. Because the stakes are high, the manner in which we deal with collegial problems can be as important as our dealings with family and friends. Once again the challenges are great, and there is much to be discovered from these experiences. We really can learn more about ourselves from our enemies than we can from our friends.

XIV ⌘ Problem-Solving Colleagues and Co-workers

1. Accepting

When you are having a problem in your work environment, accept the situation as it is, rather than what you want it to be. Objectively evaluate exactly what is going on. It may help to imagine that you have to explain the problem to a neutral third party in five minutes or less. Try to explain it without becoming defensive or trying to justify or exaggerate it. Acceptance is the opposite of illusion. It involves honest and realistic appraisals of the situation. It involves awareness of the facts without "if only's" or "maybe's". Accept that you may be wrong and your boss or colleague may have some valid points. Once you can objectively accept the problem you are having, you have moved from reacting to it to understanding it.

Try to classify the problem as an issue involving power and

control, a personality problem, or one that deals with illusions and expectations. Accept the fact that you are having this problem but that you may not be able to solve it or change it. Recognize that this problem probably will not go away quickly or easily and that you may either have to live with it or make some difficult choices. Accept the reality that working with others is always going to involve problems and that changing this situation will not lead to the perfect work environment. When this problem is resolved, others will surface. Accept this and try to put it in perspective.

2. Letting Go

In a problem relationship with a colleague, let go of your illusion that you can get along with everybody. Forget the idea you are supposed to like, trust, and be compatible with everyone you work with. Let go of the crazy idea that everyone will also like, trust, and be able to get along with you. Stop trying to be perfect. Recognize that you have your quirks, your craziness, your rigidities, and so does everyone else. Let go of the idea that having a co-worker dislike you is shameful or in some way lessens you. Stop trying to always defend yourself or justify your behavior. Let go of criticism, first of yourself and next of the problematic colleague.

Let go of your own insecure need to have others agree with you in order to feel better. In other words do not try to form a coalition of supporters of your position. Do not try to involve other co-workers in your problem. Splitting them into two camps, those for you and those against you, will only lead to more serious problems. Let go of forcing others to choose sides. Let go of the idea that your side is right and the other is wrong. Finally, let go of your need to intensify or dramatize your problem. This will result in less confrontation, less excitement, less conversation, less trauma-drama, but it will allow a solution to surface or a resolution to occur.

If you recognize that your problem concerns power and control issues, let go of any illusions of control you may have. Try to let go of your needs to have power over others—this is a sure manifestation of your weak ego. Esteem yourself and let go of needing or demanding this from your co-workers. If you are involved in a situation with lots of responsibility and little control, stop assuming the responsibility. Again, if you like to feel important, to be needed, to have others look up to you, recognize that this also reflects your insecurity, your weak ego. Let go of the training you have received that defines success by external things. Look around you at those you respect and admire and ask yourself which of them are good role models for you. If they are not internally secure, balanced, and emotionally healthy, you will probably not select them. Remember, these traits do not come from the Doing model. You can only learn them by Being, by going within.

When your problem is one of personality differences with a colleague, let go of trying to change the other. Stop taking responsibility for him without having any control over him. Let go of fantasizing how different it would be if he was not there. This will probably not occur anytime soon and is stopping you from dealing with the reality of the problem. Forget trying to appease or placate this problematic person; most likely you cannot. Stop the fight with him; this is a war you will surely lose. Try instead to separate yourself enough to be objective, to see what you are doing that can be changed, and to evaluate if and how this situation is meeting some secondary needs for you. In other words is this difficult relationship giving you attention, support, sympathy, or something else that you need from others? If so, let go and work on filling your own needs. If you are enmeshed in a sticky collegial relationship, let go and get out. No matter how painful it is at this moment, it can only get worse.

3. Expressing Feelings

Expressing feelings in your work environment is very different from doing so with friends or family. This culture and your subsequent training place high value on stoicism, showing a stiff upper lip, and controlling emotions. Nowhere are these qualities more valued than in the workplace. This is the place that values rational and logical behavior over emotionality. Here, being emotionally expressive may be labeled hysterical, moody, or out of control. Men are often labeled weak or unmasculine if they express certain emotions (they can express anger but sadness, empathy, and exuberance are more suspect if displayed effusively), and women tend to be called aggressive or difficult if they loudly express anger or dissension.

Fortunately you can learn to express your emotions in a manner that is acceptable in the work environment and still satisfies your needs to vent and release your feelings. What you feel (except about yourself) is not in your control; how you choose to express it is. This expression of your feelings is your behavior. For example, feeling anger is different from acting angry, which is the behavior. Anger does not require yelling or acting out in order to be released. Sadness and pain do not require tears in order to be acknowledged. Acknowledgment of the feeling to yourself is the important step, in order to let it go.

How you choose to share your feelings with others is secondary to the release process. In the work setting, being calm and in control while telling others how you feel is critical to solving your problem. Saying "I am upset" or "I am hurt" in a calm, sane manner can be extremely effective. This delivery style sets the tone for reasonable and productive communications to occur. In order to do this, rehearse your feelings before you present them to another. Be as emotionally expressive as you can, when you are alone. Yell and scream, rant and rage, cry and shake before you tell your co-worker what you are feeling. Get the emotion out when you are in a safe, secluded place. Then, when you are calm and feeling in control, share the feeling with the other if you feel that will be helpful. Often just expressing the feelings will be enough, and sharing is not necessary or effective. The critical issue here is to be true to yourself and to know what you are feeling when you are feeling it. You can be true to yourself without always sharing what you feel with others.

4. Taking Responsibility

This issue of power and control is extremely salient in the work environment. Here are found the hierarchies and organizational charts that define success. The concept of boss and subservient worker is based on these structures. It may be very difficult to feel powerful when you are at the bottom of such a hierarchy. It is important to recognize that this is all based on an illusion of power and control—an illusion because the attribution of power is given by those who are least powerful to those who are more powerful. Power and control are given; they cannot be demanded. And the giver has the ultimate control because he can always stop. In other words you cannot control someone who is not there to be controlled. Ultimately it is your choice, and therefore your responsibility, whom you are empowering and how you are doing so. Your personal power is comprised of how you feel about yourself (self-esteem) and how you behave. No one can take this away from you. You allow others to control you for many reasons, not the least of which is the desire to keep your job and salary. But you have the option to leave, to stop, to do something else.

It is important to recognize what is your responsibility and what is not. You might be responsible for things that are hidden or covert, such as the empowering of others or the encouragement or discouragement that affects how they behave and what control they may have. You probably know that not all bosses run the show; workers have covert roles in the organization that cannot be diagrammed on the charts. Be clean with yourself and recognize where you are exerting hidden power or control. Take responsibility for what you are doing and for part of the outcome. Do not blame others for what is really yours. If you do, you are living the illusion, perpetuating the lie, and only really fooling and hurting your Self. Why would you want to do so?

5. Forgiving

Forgiving your family and friends may be much easier than forgiving your colleagues. With the former you may choose to forgive and let go of the anger and pain because you know they will always be in your life and you want to be close and intimate with them. Or you may decide to forgive them and literally let them go and never see them again. This is a choice you cannot make with your colleagues because you will have to see them every day, even if you may wish you did not. Forgiveness is more difficult if someone is constantly nearby, repeating the very actions you are trying to forgive. This may be one of your great challenges.

One of the big traps to avoid here is that of forgiving people as a way of trying to have power over them. You cannot forgive someone for something he does not feel was wrong. You forgive what you have earlier blamed; if the other refuses to believe it is his fault or responsibility, your forgiveness will appear patronizing, condescending, or manipulative. In these cases you will forgive him for yourself, as your way of letting go and moving on. You will not force your forgiveness on him or share it with others who may do so. You will not use your forgiveness as a means of asserting superiority or of winning something. This is a very personal process, effective only when there are no ulterior motives. Forgiveness must be true, clean, and real. You are forgiving in order to be the best you can be. If the other does not want, need, or ask for your forgiveness, then sharing it with him may backfire and reverse your progress toward resolving the problem.

6. Appreciating

It is another paradox that the more difficult the problems you have in a relationship, the more difficult a person is for you to deal with, the more appreciation you can have for the opportunity to learn. You will be taught more by your enemies and troubles than you ever will from your friends and comforts. This is probably because you do not stretch yourself when you are feeling safe and secure. In order to learn something new, you must be unfamiliar, unsure, and uncomfortable. Difficult work relationships will cause you to question your values, challenge your belief systems, and discover new facets of yourself. At the very least they will teach you how not to be, what not to do, and how not to inflict similar pain on others. This is a lot to learn, and you can appreciate the other for teaching you so much about yourself. You can be thankful for the lessons you are learning even when it is difficult to appreciate the teacher. The more secure you are, the wiser you have become, the easier it will be to separate yourself from your difficult relationships and to appreciate the process, even when the context may be painful. Because you do not have the time to do and be everything in this life, you can appreciate others for helping you make your own choices, based on their experiences and behavior.

You can also appreciate the fact that your difficult work relationships can help you move off the Doing model, on which your worth is measured by externals, and into Being, where you yourself recognize your worth. If everything you did was successful, if all your relationships worked well, and if your trip up the ladder of success was fairly simple, you would have little incentive to change models. The fall from the top is much more traumatic and painful than the fall from a lower rung. Your difficulties now will help you avoid later and greater pain. You can surely appreciate that!

7. Rewarding

Reward your colleagues by being the best person you can be at work. You can do this by being a team player, understanding that sometimes the whole is more important than your individual ego. You can set aside your own needs for the good of all, and you can share in the glory. Reward those you work with by noticing and complimenting them when they do well, by giving respect for their contributions, and by treating your colleagues as you yourself would like to be treated. Reward the person who is giving you a problem by saying something genuinely and honestly nice about him. Everyone has something he does well; everyone has something that can be complimented. Be honest and express something positive that you really believe. A positive reward can overcome a great deal of negativity. It cannot change everything, but negativity breeds discouragement, and all of us need more encouragement. Saying something positive, doing something kind, sharing our goodness, are all encouraging activities and they lead to a rewarding environment.

Reward yourself for being in a difficult situation and trying to make the best of it. Especially reward yourself for surviving, persevering, and trying to do the best you can. When your environment is the least rewarding, you must be even more rewarding to yourself. Remember, the rewards you give yourself are yours to keep. The external ones, the ones that everybody is competing for and fighting over, are, at best, temporary and usually not very meaningful or important in the whole picture. Only you know what you really need when you most need it; reward yourself by giving yourself what you need whenever you can. You may not be able to give yourself society's definitions of achievement—wealth, power, influence, and recognition by others—but you can give yourself what you really need—esteem, love, kindness, respect, and awareness that you are doing the best job possible. These are the things that ultimately count, that reflect the reality of a successful life.

*Let your light so shine before men, that
they may see your good works, and glorify
your Father which is in Heaven.*

—Matthew 5:16

XV ⌁ The Self

Finally we come to the critical relationship and the one that is responsible for most of our difficulties in life—our relationship with the Self. This is the only one we will ever have in which we hold all the control and power. Ironically this is the one that we generally know the least about, and on which we typically focus the least amount of time and effort. In order to become problem solvers, we will need to refocus our energy away from others and onto ourselves.

During the preceding pages describing the problems that may be encountered in relationships with others, hopefully we may have recognized some things that have applied directly to us. As mentioned in the introduction to this book, we have relationships in order to learn about ourselves. Our interactions with others can be used as mirrors for self-awareness and self-knowledge. Our families and friends can help us to dispel our illusions about ourselves and to help us recognize who and what we really are. While this is important information to have, most of us are aware that it is not enough as a basis for self-acceptance or for change.

Faulty Training

Somewhere around the age of twenty we begin to be accountable and responsible for who we are and what we do. We have progressed into the "adult" stage of life, and most of our training about how to be stops. We may continue to receive training about what to do, but there is no longer any formal training about being. (As a matter of fact there is not a lot of formal training about being at any stage in our lives; unless we have been very lucky with parents, teachers, and other role models, most of us are lacking in the constructs of being.) Our society in general does not deal with the developmental stages that continue to occur in adulthood. Our culture is lacking when it comes to lifelong education about the art of being. It is no wonder, then, that a very tiny minority of us have any idea about how to have a good relationship with the Self.

The Difficulty with Self-esteem

At the heart of this relationship with the self is the way that we perceive the Self; *self-esteem* can be defined as a positive concept, while *insecurity* means a negative self-image. The importance of a good self-relationship has clearly been recognized, as hundreds of books and articles dealing with helping and improving oneself have been written in the past few decades. And millions of people have read at least one of these publications. Countless others have attended seminars or workshops dealing with this topic. And yet the practice of true self-esteem is still very rare. For the most part the books are good, the seminars are good, the message is out there, but the practice of loving ourselves is not really understood. Why? Is this concept so difficult, so complex, so abstract that it cannot be communicated to others? Perhaps the construct of "self-esteem" is like the construct of "peace"; both have been talked about so much that we tend to give them lip service only. We know that both ideas are good—we have been flooded with their merit—but we do not know how to take them from their pervasive and rather abstract plateaux into the reality of our minute-to-minute lives. We say we desire peace as we fight with our nearest and dearest; we say we want self-esteem as we walk around feeling guilty, selfish, bad, and anxious. We quickly give up the idea of peace as soon as we feel threatened; we just as easily give up our self-esteem as soon as something goes wrong. We blame rather than accept; we find discouragement more familiar than encouragement. And we double the blame and discouragement in our relationship with the Self. It is no wonder that we feel overwhelmed by our problems, beginning with the essential problem of who we are.

The Beginning of Self-Discovery

Fortunately there is a way to solve the problem of self-discovery. It is simple, practical, and it works! But it is not easy. In order to begin, we must want the relationship with the Self. And we must be willing to dedicate some time, energy, and effort to the discovery process. In the initial phases this may feel like a lot of work and will involve some pain and confusion. We may have already discovered that this is true of all relationships. The biggest difference here—in the relationship we have with ourselves—is that this is the one we can keep, the only one we can control, the most important relationship we will ever have in our lives. As a matter of fact this is the relationship that defines our lives. Ultimately it is our life.

To begin the process of self-discovery, it is critical to understand that there is a difference between the person we present to the world (the outer self) and the person we keep hidden (the inner self). Once we have developed a good relationship with ourselves, this difference disappears and the outer and inner selves become one and the same. This is defined as a balanced or whole, evolved or centered person. Those who have integrated the outer and inner selves are our role models, our "gurus," and they serve to show that this can be achieved.

The External Self

The outer self, or facade, is what we tend to know best about ourselves because this is the one the world has taught us to be. This outward manifestation of "me" is what we have been developing throughout our lifetime. Because it is a product of our training, which has essentially been done by others, this self is comprised of being and doing what they want us to be and do;

this explains why this outer self is comprised of our "weak ego," our appearance and our externals. Our outer self is dependent upon others to define us. It has been created to impress those around us, in order to fulfill our own needs. The "weak ego" is defined as the part of us that derives its worth and esteem from the externals—those things outside ourselves and therefore outside our control. That is why it is weak, because at any moment, since they depend on someone or something else, our esteem and worth can disappear. If a loved one stops loving us, if we are fired from our job, if we lose everything in a flood or fire, the outer self is devastated. Even without the trauma of life, if we count on our appearance or external traits to define our worth, we also become devastated as we age and change.

The Internal Self

The inner self is comprised of our self-esteem, inner child, dark side, soul (our relationship with God) and spirit (our spiritual relationships with others), and our own goodness, which can also be described as our relationship with God. It is not dependent on anyone or anything else. It is solely dependent on how we feel about our Self, and our own recognition and active awareness of who we are in there. It is this Self that we alone can control. It is this Self that determines whether we have a sense of identity, understand the real meaning of success and worth, experience joy, and live life to the fullest. This is the side of ourselves that determines what our life is, has been, and will be. It is this side that is connected to the Whole, understands belongingness, and feels the beauty and meaning of life. This is the part of us that fills the emptiness and makes sense of the problems. This is our completion, our totality, our meaning, and our connection. This is where the answers are found and the challenges are met. If we do not know this internal side, the best we can hope to be is a shadow of our possibility.

The Paradox of Control

One of the great ironies in life is that we are trained to juxtapose the relationship between the Self that we can control and the one we cannot. We have been taught to control the outer self, which we cannot do, as it is dependent on external things, while we ignore the inner self, which we can control. We spend huge amounts of time working on our physical appearance and little to no time on what is going on inside. If we would only worry half as much about the state of the inner self as we do about the outer self—our looks, sexuality, and how others perceive us—we would all have self-esteem and healthy relationships with ourselves. Working on our interiors means spending some time alone each day focusing on what we are feeling, needing, missing, and then doing something about them. It means consistently checking in with the Self and making it a daily priority to take care of ourselves. There are many ways in which to do this—meditating; keeping a journal; attending to the inner child by satisfying our basic needs; talking and listening to the Self; doing creative activities, such as painting, dancing, sculpting, playing music—all of which lend themselves to the practice of self-awareness. There are also activities that take very little time but are highly effective—looking in the mirror and saying "I love you" or "You are good!", patting yourself on the back, paying yourself a compliment, hugging yourself when you need a hug.

The critical distinction to understand in the process of developing self-worth is the recognition that the outer self is almost always involved with others, while the inner self is only concerned with us. In other words we take our inner selves with us wherever we go. We may not be as fully aware of our inner selves as we are our outer ones, but we cannot leave the former behind. We can, and often do, shed the facade—the outer self—when we are alone. We can never shed our interiors. Furthermore we can never control our exteriors in the way that we can our inner selves, because our external sides are dependent upon others. Since we can only control ourselves, and never others, our inner selves are the part over which we exert total control. We cannot completely control our appearances, how others perceive us, or how they feel about us. And yet, by God, how hard we try! What we can control are the direction of our changes, our own development and growth, our feelings of worth and personal power, and our behavior. We can control who we are and what we are, but only when we work on our inner selves. Why, then, are we a nation of overworked and overstressed outer selves and undervalued and unknown inner selves?

Using What We Know

We cannot discard our outer selves, nor would we want to, but we can use the knowledge of how we have developed our facades to help us become aware of our inner selves. We can use the ways in which we relate with others in order to learn how to relate to ourselves. As mentioned, we begin by wanting this relationship. When we really want it, we will be willing to spend time, money, effort, and energy on it. Remember, all our other relationships function as a means of learning about ourselves. Therefore we can use all of them as models for this relationship. If the first step in doing so is to want, the second step is to care. When we make the decision that we are worthy of being loved and then act accordingly, we begin to treat ourselves as we treat those we love.

When we begin to love someone else, what do we do? We say nice things to him (or her). We behave in caring, nurturing, and protective ways toward him. We do favors for him and we give him gifts. We pay him lots of compliments. We accept him as an imperfect being and we encourage him when he needs it. We forgive him his mistakes and we acknowledge his feelings and his right to have those feelings. We are loving.

Learning How to Be

Now *do all these things for the Self*. In other words we can now do for ourselves exactly what we are willing to do for those we love. Moreover we can do these things for ourselves *before* we do them for anyone else. We can be kind and gentle to our Selves. We can pay attention to our needs and attend to them. We can parent our inner child just as we would parent any beloved child who is in pain. We can try listening to ourselves. We can trust our instincts and honor our feelings without trying to justify them. Above all we can recognize our innate goodness. Then and only then can we lower our expectations and praise our accomplishments. We can try to get rid of our illusions by making our own realities more loving. We have to get rid of the destructive illusion that we will ever be perfect. We can practice laughing at our mistakes and accepting our own idiosyncrasies. We can recognize that we learn from everything that is difficult and unwanted in our lives. We can become aware that our presents from God are usually disguised as unwanted problems. Our responses and solutions to our problems are in reality the development of the inner self and the beginning of our character.

The Fear of Self-esteem

At this point we may begin to wonder if doing all the above will make us narcissistic. All of us have met egoists who seem to do everything for themselves, with little concern for others. This is not what we want to become. We do not have to worry, because there is a critical difference between being egocentric and having self-esteem. The former requires, and usually de-mands, others to be involved in one's self-adoration. These unfortunate ones are actually demonstrating huge weak egos. The process of loving the Self is done alone. We do not need to have an audience or to convince anyone else of our worth. As a matter of fact the more we are convinced of our value and the more we love ourselves, the less we need others to value and esteem us. Self-esteemed ones paradoxically seem to others to be quite humble, as their needs for adoration and adulation have been fulfilled by themselves. Egocentric ones, those with weak egos, on the other hand, talk and bluster as if they are the greatest beings around. Ironically if they really believed what they are trying to convince others to believe, they would have no need for the big show. They would use the time they spend impressing others in taking care of themselves. Loving the Self is a quiet activity. When we do so, we quickly recognize that we are not the center of anything except our own Self. And that is enough.

The Process

Above everything else, recognize that loving the Self is process. We never arrive in this lifetime, we never complete, we never achieve a problem-free state and keep it. Therefore we continue to practice, practice, practice. Practice acceptance. Practice rewarding the Self. Practice encouragement. Practice being human. Practice being a problem solver.

This practicing is living. This is what life is for and what it is about. We are truly on a journey of which we cannot know the end. Because of this we need to be aware that the journey becomes the end, that what we do and what we are give meaning to the travel. It is true that we did not initially create our Selves, but it is also true that we do create our lives and we do create the changes within ourselves. Because we do not know for sure what the ending might be, it is up to us to focus on what we can know and what we do control. When we recognize this, we perceive that there is a marvelous simplicity to the whole process. When we try to live in the content and context of external life, we quickly become overwhelmed by the complexity of it all. But when we remain aware of the process and invest our energies and time on what is within our control, we simplify and understand.

We cannot make sense of what we do not know and will never comprehend; we can make sense of our Selves and our own lives. The only way to do so is to focus on what we have within our control—the way we feel about ourselves and our behavior, based on these feelings. Paradoxically by focusing on our Self, we make sense of it all. When we learn self-esteem and practice it, we automatically learn social interest. We become spiritual beings when we recognize the goodness within ourselves and acknowledge the goodness in others. This process of recognition and acknowledgment of goodness leads to the practice of encouragement, which then becomes the reality of living the "good life." We can create in ourselves and in our world a place that is loving, affirming, and spiritual; this, then, becomes the world we live in.

XVI ∾ Problem-Solving the Self

1. Accepting

Accept who you are, right now, just as you are, warts and all. This can be extremely difficult, as you have been trained to focus on what you are going to be after you change. Acceptance is not about change. Forget how you are going to change and take a good look at the reality of yourself at this moment. Stand naked in front of a mirror and look at yourself for a long time. (No, you will not go blind!) Keep looking until you lose yourself—until you can see yourself objectively. Get past the things that you do not like—get past the fat, the bumps, and the imperfections. Look long enough until you can begin to perceive what is underneath the outer self, until you gain a sense of your interior self. Look at yourself with loving eyes, until you can feel the love for yourself. Recognize that your exterior often hides you from your true beauty.

Accept yourself as good. You are good, but all your training has worked to negate or deny your innate goodness. Tell yourself, "I am good!" Keep saying it until you feel it, until you recognize the truth in this statement. This is usually very powerful and you will know when you feel it, when you believe it. At this time you may feel like crying; please do so. These will be welcome tears of joy for discovering your lost Self.

Accept yourself as flawed. You can never be perfect. You are not supposed to be perfect. It is okay to be imperfect. You are supposed to be what you are, right now! You are supposed to be where you are, doing what you are doing and feeling whatever you are feeling. Accept this. It is your reality and your challenge. Whatever problems you may have, you are supposed to have. Accept them. Accept the fact that your problems are teaching you to be a problem solver and are allowing you to develop your character. Your difficulties are exercises for your soul, and the more challenging they are, the more you will be stretched. Just as you need to exercise your body (exterior) to become healthy and flexible, so also do you need to exercise your spirit (interior).

2. Letting Go

Just as you have let go of the idea that anyone else can ever be perfect, now let go of the dangerous illusion that you can be perfect. This is hard. You have been trained to try to achieve perfection. Let go of your training. It will only lead you to depression, frustration, and mental illness. You cannot strive for an impossible goal and end up being whole. Remember, most of those who have committed suicide have done so because they felt they were "no good"; they confused goodness with perfection. Do not make this fatal mistake.

Let go of beating yourself up. You denigrate yourself with guilt and anxiety and "shoulds." You lessen yourself when you try to be something you are not. You abuse yourself when you are "hard" on yourself, when you demand more from yourself, when you criticize and discourage yourself, and when you engage in negativity. Just as you cannot be perfect, you also cannot be a perfect failure.

Let go of judging. Let go of comparisons. Your worth is not determined relative to anyone else's worth. Your life is not a contest or a competition. Let go of the pressure to succeed. Your success in this life cannot be determined by others, or by society. It can only be determined by how you feel about your Self. If you love yourself, if you behave in loving ways, if you recognize your goodness, you are a success.

Let go of negativity. Stop hating. Let go of the idea that life can be fair. It is not fair and it will never be fair. Let go of your need to control what you cannot control. You cannot control others, so you might as well stop trying. You are not responsible for what you cannot control; why would you want to take this on? If you recognize that this is an impossible task, why attempt it? Letting go will allow you to breathe, to focus on what you can do, and to begin the process of Being. Let go of worrying about anything that you cannot do something about right now. Let go of your fears. Most of your fears are out of your control and involve things that you cannot do anyway. Do what you can, take risks, and let go of the need for control that is paralyzing you.

Let go of the concept that life is about Doing. Learn instead that life is about Being. Do less. Be more. Let go of the notion that if something is wrong, you have to do more in order to fix it. As a matter of fact let go of the idea that you can fix everything. You cannot. Some things fix themselves, some things cannot be fixed at all. Problem solving is not about fixing. Oftentimes it is about accepting. And many times it is about letting go.

3. Expressing Feelings

In this relationship it is critical to express positive feelings to yourself. This may sound weird and the practice may initially be quite difficult, as it goes against your lifelong training. Begin every morning and end every day by saying "I love you" to yourself. A good way to remember to do this is to look in the mirror and say it every time you brush your teeth. Sounds silly? Try it. At first it will feel strange or uncomfortable, but keep at it. One day you will feel loved and this is the only love in the world that you can control. It is simply impossible to love yourself without expressing that love to yourself.

Express your feelings to yourself as they occur. Give them permission to be. After all, you cannot control them, but you can allow them to exist and be released. If you have difficulties with emotions, practice saying, "I am feeling _____ and it is okay." Feeling is being; acting on it is doing. You do not have to act, to behave, every time you have a feeling. Just because you do not have control over your feelings does not mean that you have to let them control you. You do have control over your behavior—your expression of your emotions—and you can have feelings without being out of control. The manner in which you express your emotions is your choice and is in your control. Once you have learned this distinction between having a feeling and acting on it (behaving), you will never have to fear your emotions again.

Say nice things to yourself. You are choosing to feel good about yourself; you can also choose to express positive or negative thoughts about what you do. Whenever you can, choose the positive. Say, "That was good," "I did well," "I liked that," or "That felt good," whenever the occasion warrants the praise. When you make mistakes, admit them and let them go. Express your feelings about being wrong and move on. Try not to get stuck in the negativity from your training. Practice changing "I am so stupid" or "I am bad" into "I made a mistake" or "I don't like what I did." Acknowledge your error and move on to the next steps.

Pat yourself on the back every night just before you fall asleep. Think about something that you did today that you liked and give yourself a pat for it. Express to yourself your satisfaction for your deed, no matter how small. If there is absolutely nothing you feel good about, then pat yourself for surviving such a terrible day. Do this little exercise without fail every night of your life. Praising yourself, expressing positive feelings to yourself, being good to yourself are critical to feeling good about yourself. You are learning encouragement, and you will need a lot of it in order to overcome your discouraging training.

4. Taking Responsibility

Take responsibility for your life. It is yours and yours alone. Take the blame for how you feel about yourself and how you behave. Take responsibility for the part of your problems that you can control. Then do something about them. Take responsibility for changing. You are the only person who can change yourself. If you learned something and it no longer works for you, relearn it and do it differently. You are not stuck unless you let yourself be. You are not static, but rather are constantly changing even if you do not recognize this. Control your own change. Move in a positive direction and change for the better. Seek help, find support, but recognize that the ultimate responsibility is to yourself.

Own your own weak ego. This is the reason for your insecurities and it is a part of you that you can learn to control. Your training has taught you to believe that your esteem and value come from externals. It has fed your weak ego and made it strong and powerful. As soon as you take responsibility for your weak ego, you begin to take control of it. Practicing self-esteem is the best way to keep your weak ego under control; satisfying your own needs means less dependence upon the externals for gratification. You will never entirely get rid of your weak ego, you will never be completely free from your weaknesses (you will never become perfect!), but you can minimize the power of the weak ego by esteeming yourself and taking responsibility for what is yours.

Do not take responsibility for what you cannot control. Do not waste your time and energy on trying to change or control others. You simply cannot.

5. Forgiving

Forgive yourself for everything you have ever done wrong, for every mistake you have made, for all the parts of yourself you do not like, for your negativity, and for your imperfections. Forgive yourself for your bad actions and your wicked thoughts. Forgive yourself for your weak ego and self-centeredness. Forgive yourself for being unkind and for not caring. Forgive yourself for whatever bothers you about yourself. Forgive yourself, let go, and move on.

Forgiving yourself is not the same as excusing yourself. When you excuse your actions, you tend to justify and repeat them. Forgiveness implies really feeling sorry and has a strong connection with repentance. Forgive yourself and try not to repeat whatever has been forgiven. If you feel bad enough about something to need forgiveness, then you will learn by remembering how bad you feel and by planning to do something different the next time. You forgive yourself not as a way of continuing negative behavior but as a way of moving past it to the positive. Acting in a loving, encouraging, nurturing manner never requires forgiveness. You will always have something to forgive because you can never be perfect, but you can strive toward doing less of the things that require forgiveness.

Do not forgive yourself for things that were not your fault. Forgive others for what was their responsibility, their behavior, their negativity and insecurity. You cannot forgive yourself for the bad things that others have done to you. You cannot be forgiven without being blamed. If you were victimized or abused by someone else, you do not need to forgive yourself, but you will need to forgive your victimizer or abuser, in order to be free of him or her. Forgiveness implies responsibility and control. Only forgive yourself for what is yours to forgive.

6. Appreciating

Appreciate what you are, what you have to give, and your uniqueness. Give thanks for being you. You cannot do this unless you really love your Self. Once you love yourself, you can appreciate your worth and contributions. Appreciate the gifts that you give others, especially when they themselves do not appreciate them. The gifts you give have much more to do with you than with the recipient. Appreciate that you give, that you care, that you are trying. Appreciate that your life is difficult and that you have problems. Your difficulties, your problems, and your overcoming them have allowed you to become what you are. Facing the challenges of life *is* life. A life without difficulty would hold no opportunity for becoming stronger, for learning, and for growing. Life without conflict would be boring and would lead to stagnation. Appreciate that your life is certainly not boring, and if it is, that is your problem, a challenge you can solve. Appreciate that you are a problem solver and that you have whatever it takes to do what you want to do.

Finally, appreciate your goodness. It is a gift from God. By appreciating this great gift, you will open yourself to the goodness around you, and allow others to become aware of their goodness. Appreciate that by practicing self-love you are also allowing others to do the same. You are being spiritual, as you are recognizing the goodness within yourself, which then allows you to acknowledge the goodness in others. Thank God for all this goodness; God and good are one and the same.

7. Rewarding

Rewarding yourself can be defined as fulfilling your own needs. You give to yourself what you would like others to give to you. You give these things because you deserve them. You take care of your own needs because you are the only person who can. After all, you are the only one who knows exactly what you want and need, precisely when you want and need it. As soon as you know, take care of the need. If you need support, be supportive of yourself. If you need praise, give yourself praise. When you do something well, reward yourself by acknowledging that you have done a good job.

Do not worry about sounding conceited or being selfish. You are being selfish if you define selfishness as taking care of the self. There is nothing wrong with this. Bragging or sounding conceited requires the presence of others. Taking care of yourself does not. Telling yourself that you are great is quite different from telling others how great you are. The latter is a means of seeking approval from others; the former is giving approval to your Self. When others are involved in fulfilling your needs, you are a victim of your own weak ego. Self-esteem means that you are doing for yourself what your weak ego would like others to do for you.

Give yourself your own rewards. They are the only ones that last. When others reward you, it is the icing on the cake. But you are the cake, and a really good cake does not need icing. The rewards others give us can make life sweeter, but they cannot make life real or meaningful. External rewards are always temporary; the only ones that last are the ones that nourish your soul. These are the rewards you give yourself. Be soulful; reward yourself so that you can then reward the world by your very being.

*We have learned to be citizens of the
world, members of the human community.*

—FRANKLIN D. ROOSEVELT

XVII ~ The Community

Social interest can be defined as the way we relate with others
when we have self-esteem. We simply apply toward others what
we have learned to do for ourselves in the process of developing
self-worth. We have learned to love ourselves as imperfect beings; now we will practice this with our other relationships. This
may seem easier to do in our relationships with family, lovers,
and friends than it is with the community, those with whom we
are not intimate. Perhaps this is because we are more familiar
with and dependent upon those in close proximity to us. However, the relationships we have with the community, extending
to the world at large, are just as critical in defining who we are
and how we live as are our more intimate ones. The difficulties
we have and the problems we encounter in our relationships
with the community are usually caused by a lack of acceptance
and understanding. The reason we cannot accept or relate with
others is usually founded in differing value systems; these conflicting systems serve to separate and differentiate us from
others.

Training and Environment

We have been taught to compare ourselves with and judge others and to think in terms of dichotomies—similarities or differences. We learn to like, and therefore accept and trust, those who are similar and to distrust those who are not. When we perceive others as different from us, it is usually because they believe or value things that conflict with what we have been taught. What we tend to forget is that what we believe and value and how we relate with others are learned behaviors, taught to us by those with concepts similar to ours. Our value systems often become the basis for problems we have in relating to the community and to the world. As soon as we are able to move beyond the boundaries of these learned values, we quickly recognize the similarities that exist in all of us. If we cannot move past our restrictive systems, we remain alienated and convinced that we cannot relate to those whom we label as different.

There is an ongoing controversy in the sciences regarding how much of our behavior and characteristics are due to genetics (nature) and how much can be attributed to environmental factors (nurture). Our relationship with the world, based on perceived similarities or differences, is probably the one problem area entirely developed from our training and environment. There is very little, if any, nature involved in the development of our value systems, in spite of the fact that most of us might think that this is one of the areas that most define who we really are. It is certainly the single most consistently passionate arena for our problems and therefore one of the most difficult to deal with in our relationships. Because we possess the marvelous human tendency to believe intensely whatever it is that we value at the moment, we often forget that these values are not immutable. What we choose to value at a particular time in our lives is not the totality of who or what we are. We change our values with or without conscious awareness as we develop and mature. Therefore at different stages in our lives we believe different concepts and adhere to different values. And yet we generally consider these systems to be fixed, constant, and rigid.

Learning Our Value System

Developmentally we begin with nothing except the will to survive. This results in attachment to mother or the primary caretaker; it does not take too long before we, as young children, attach not only to mother, but also to what mother believes or values. She is right because she is life. We need her approval, so we will agree with her to make her happy and ultimately make us happy as well, or keep us alive, fed, and protected. It is really just that simple. We extend this reciprocity to all parental figures, older siblings, and caregivers. What they consider good becomes our definition of goodness; what they label as bad defines bad for us. It is all we know.

As we develop language, the process intensifies. As soon as we understand what they are saying, we get a very good idea of what they are thinking. Parents and family are the center of the world at this point, and what they tell us becomes "right," becomes our worldview. Because we are individuals striving for some degree of autonomy and independence, we will test some of their ideas some of the time, beginning around two years of age. But for the most part what they say is what we hear, and what they believe becomes what we know. We learn to walk and talk, feel and think, act and react because we are genetically programmed to do so. However, what we think and say and what we learn to believe are dependent on the environment. This process is known as acculturation. Thus even our choices of how we act and react are largely programmed from our surroundings and conform to cultural values.

We learn quickly and pick up on all the available clues. We become aware of what our parents believe and value, what their biases are, and whom they like and dislike before we ever enter school. We think that they are right because they are our ultimate authority. School challenges this for us. We meet others who think differently, but share our belief that our respective parents are absolutely right. Part of this certainty comes from language and part from our human need for order and structure in the world. Language is generally linear, in that it forces us to think dichotomously (good or bad, right or wrong, up or down, black or white). By doing so it imposes superficial or nonexistent boundaries upon our mental processes in order for us to make sense of what we know and to communicate with others. Our need to create order out of chaos and to structure our world into manageable constructs creates more boundaries and limitations in our thinking. This is what we must do in order to make sense of it all. There is nothing wrong with bounding and limiting in order to make life manageable, unless we forget that we are doing so. Problems occur when we are not aware that these structured boundaries are artificial ones and that our created limitations are indeed limiting. We tend to forget that we have conceived some type of order to try to structure and manage our world, to prevent chaos. More important, we learn to dislike anyone who disagrees with or threatens what we have done. In actuality we have created emotional distance and the beginnings of community conflict from our desire to prevent chaos, protect our beliefs, and feel secure within our constructs. The same boundaries that help us manage our world are the ones that alienate and separate, confine and constrict, us from becoming close to those with different systems and worldviews.

Intensity of Belief

As we grow, change, and mature, our values change along with us. But at the very moment when we are defending what we so passionately believe, we also forget that this is not what we believed before, and may not be what we will believe in the future. Interestingly the thing that does not seem to change across time is the degree of intensity we give to the expression of our beliefs. Thus many of the extreme radicals of the sixties have become the extreme conservatives of the nineties. Perhaps this intensity, the degree to which we feel strongly, is genetic, even though the values themselves are learned. It is easier to change what is learned or environmentally produced than what is innate and wired in. Our ability to be passionate may be inherited or it may be culturally learned or reinforced; probably it is some combination of both. What we care deeply about is not inherited, but clearly culturally conditioned and rewarded. In other words our ability to feel is innate, and the degree to which we express our feelings may well be a combination of inborn temperament and cultural learning, but the choice of what we are passionate about is environmentally induced. Our choices will not always be the same things that produce passion in those who have been exposed to different value systems and feel just as intensely about their learned constructs. We all believe and value, in varying degrees, what our culture respects and teaches. We all ardently feel that our value systems are an important part of defining who we are; when we face different systems, we perceive them as clear demarcations for separation. It is much easier to stress the differences; it can be difficult and quite challenging to seek the similarities.

When we were children, we usually believed that our parents were invincible and could solve all problems. When we became adolescents, we found this was not so. As we moved into adulthood, we frequently felt more powerful than they. We were often convinced that what we knew is correct and that our parents were wrong. When we move into maturity, we find that we know less and less about more and more. At each stage of our development our value system is appropriate if it functions to help us feel secure and stable and to provide a sense of belonging within our cultural group. There is nothing wrong with any of this, unless we begin to believe that our values are the only ones that matter. Our systems function to create a sense of who we are, based on what we believe and consider important. As our needs change, so do our systems. If we can accept this, then it becomes easier to accept that others' systems function in the same way for them, and also change as they change. If our values change, and the values of others also change, why do we need to find fixed or stable ones? Why do we try to prove the validity, the rightness, of ours versus theirs?

The Difficulties Emerge

Problems with different value systems begin when we want others to believe and value what we do. When we try to make others agree with us, we create conflict. We want others to believe as we do in order to confirm that our values are correct. When they do so, we feel stronger, surer, and more powerful. We think that what we value must be right because others feel the same. This process, known as consensual validation, simply means that we have found group agreement. It does not mean that we are right or that we have discovered "the truth." Our values become related to our insecurities when we try to force others to believe as we do, in order to be comfortable with our own ideas. When we are truly secure, we are willing to allow others to think differently from us. When we are not secure, different value systems will threaten us and cause us to become either defensive or aggressive. The need to convert others to our own values is a sign of insecurity and not a mark of strength. But this is not what we have been taught. We have learned to equate strength with certainty and power. We want to believe that we know the truth, that what we value is right, and that we are special, enlightened, aware, and correct. In order to do so, we must convince others that we *know* and that they must learn from us. If others feel, as they usually do, that they know and that their knowledge is correct, and we both try to inflict our awareness upon each other, we are going to have serious problems in our community relationships.

The Problem with Choice

We cannot exist without having value systems and without feeling strongly about them. All systems, including value-laden ones, imply choices; therefore it would be impossible for any of us to try to encompass or embrace all possibilities. We are what we are, and we value what we value. This is not the problem. All others are what they are, also valuing what they do. This is also not the problem. Only when what others believe becomes a threat or a concern to us does the trouble begin. Even if we are very secure in our own value systems and try not to inflict them upon others, we are going to be confronted and challenged when others try to inflict theirs upon us. The ideal concept of living and letting live becomes almost impossible when others deliberately try to hurt or harm us or those we love. Therefore it is overly simplistic to state that we can all believe as we choose and let others do the same. As long as there are those who think that life is without meaning, that property is worth more than life, and that what they want is more important than the harm it may cause to another, our value systems and the right for conflicting beliefs to exist are going to be continual problems for us.

Because evil does exist in this world, we cannot always avoid making choices that lead to serious conflicts. We cannot change the world. We cannot stop the evil. We cannot convert anyone who is not willing to be converted. This does not mean that we do not have positive choices. The development of our values begins in early childhood and continues throughout our lives. We choose what we value, what we hold dear, what we will fight for or against, depending upon our training (the cultural model), religion, family and friends, and sometimes our own instincts. We are reinforced in these choices when those around us believe the same. We tend to gravitate toward those who are similar, in order to be confirmed and validated. Consensual validation creates a closed circle of values that seem to be "right" or "true" because no one in the circle is disagreeing or questioning. The larger the consensual circle, the greater the truth seems to be. When an entire culture or a large segment of society embraces the same values, there seems to be even more justification for believing that this is the only way to think or act. Opposition is not well tolerated, giving even more reinforcement to the worth of the concept. Thus our system may be based on an illusion, or may be outdated, or may simply not be correct or meaningful in the light of all relevant facts (which are never discussed because of the punishing of nonbelievers). Yet our self-confirmed beliefs continue to exist, to gain status, and to seem to be the absolute or only way to believe. When this occurs, monumental and destructive societal problems frequently follow. Recent mass suicides by members of religious sects are unfortunate examples of this destructive consensual thinking taken to its extreme. Discrimination based on race, religion, creeds or any external factors is another example of destructive consensual beliefs that "we are right, or okay, or better than them, and they are lesser or not as good as us."

Facade Versus Foundation

Our personal values can create many difficulties for us, especially when they are based upon illusions and expectations. What we often do not realize is that our value systems can imprison us unless we become open, flexible, and aware of changes that are constantly occurring. We become imprisoned when we create a facade for ourselves, meaning that we present only our best side to the world and keep the other side, the dark side, hidden. All facades are unidimensional in that they provide an artificial or superficial representation of reality. If we can see around one, it is readily apparent just how slight and inconsequential it really is. If our personal values are concerned with appearances, then we will feel thin and empty on the inside. Because facades are one-sided, they require a great deal of hidden support to keep them in place. We expend a huge amount of energy trying to support them, which leaves us exhausted, empty, and unable to work on the true foundation of Self.

What we really believe about the Self is much more critical than what others see or believe. Thus our foundation must be built on realistic and constructive truths about our own value and worth. For example if we believe that being a good parent is the most important thing we can do, but we do not really feel that we do it well, we may try to create the appearance of good parenting and erect a facade to fool others. We may dress our

children well, send them to the right schools, buy them whatever they want, and carry around pictures to show them off. But
if we are not consistently providing them with the love, support,
discipline, energy, and time that all children need, our facade
will not fool either them or us. We will know that we are not
doing the best we can, and our children will know it. The world
may be fooled, but the people who matter will only be hurt.
Whatever we believe about ourselves, in order to function as
foundation, must be based on the reality that at this moment we
are doing the best we can. Just as good parenting is about internal and unseen qualities, and not about external appearances, so
also are all the valuable qualities of the Self based on internal
characteristics. If we know that we are good, our beliefs about
ourselves will generally be positive ones. If we think we are bad
or lack worth, our self-beliefs will reflect this negativity, even if
we spend all our time trying to impress others and keep them
from knowing our darkest secret. It is ironic that we often spend
incredible amounts of time trying to impress others with our
facades when the concept of true community is based on strong
foundations of the collective selves and the willingness to be real
and to accept the realities of ourselves and others.

Our foundations are composed of much more than what we
value and believe, although these things are a part of our interior selves. Our foundation, the reality of who we are, is unique
to us. If we are secure in what we value and our foundation is
solid and constructively supporting the totality of us, agreement
from others is not necessary. If we have a facade instead of a
foundation, all the agreement in the world will not give us
enough support. The weak ego demands validation from others,

but when it receives it, throws the validation away or counts it meaningless. Others cannot build our foundation. It is amazing, then, to think of how much time, energy, and focus is spent on trying to impress others in order to fill our own needs. If we value the appearance of goodness more than the being or doing of good, we will focus on creating that appearance for others to see. We will not spend the time on recognizing the good within us. If we are concerned with facade rather than reality (foundation), we will value the superficial over the real, the appearance more than the actuality, and the impressing of others instead of taking care of the Self. Moreover we will value those who think the same as us and despise those who challenge or threaten us. In this way we will actually use our values to preserve the facade, thus perpetuating the power of the lie (the unreal, unknown, and unexplored) and becoming vulnerable to the destructive side within ourselves and others. To do so is to risk becoming evil, for the veneration of the facade means that the goodness within cannot be revealed. We compound this when we try to force others to do the same. When we are unable to be spiritual—to love our Selves and to perceive the goodness in others—we are putting the community at risk. Each of us is responsible for being encouraging, for recognizing the goodness that is inherent in all. Each of us is also responsible when we do not do so.

The Reality of Community

Everyone is struggling in some fashion with these issues. All of us, everywhere in the world, are dealing with our belief and value systems and the conflicts they cause in getting along with others. The process of working through these conflicts and problems is the same one for all, even though the content and context for difficulties may be very different. A second important similarity is that the journey within, the search to find our Selves and the true meaning of our lives, is difficult for everyone. No one has an easier time of this than anyone else. The illusions that surround us, the myths we believe, the fantasies we hold dear, can often separate and divide us from discovering this truth. The journey within is hard, and nothing external to us will make it easier. Our race, religion, culture, and values will not serve us well if we are contrasting and comparing them to others in the belief that we have more difficulties because of who we are. We cannot change the externals of our lives; we cannot become someone else because we think his or her journey is easier. We cannot confuse the external assets—wealth, beauty, education, success, fame, or race—with our internal work.

These external attributes function to separate us from others by focusing on the differences between us and them. Social interest is about moving past these superficial (but powerful) differences into the discovery of the great similarities we all share. The best way to do this is to focus on the process rather than the content or context of our lives. This may sound very simple, but it requires moving to a higher level of awareness. It means expanding those very boundaries that have given us security and a sense of belonging. This entails moving away from the small, safe place that defines us into a broader, more uncertain arena, in which we can easily become lost and afraid. This is a very difficult thing to do and requires great self-esteem and inner security.

We can only recognize our connection to the world when we are able to let go of our rigidities and limits, those very things that once supported us and gave us a sense of security. We can only become part of the bigger Whole when we are able to let go of our attachment to the familiar. The journey within is a prerequisite for the unification and connection to all. We must know who we are and value ourselves before we can undertake the experience of community, the discovery that we are all similar, we are all One.

XVIII ∾ Problem-Solving the Community

1. Accepting

Different problems require different solutions; this may well be the critical answer for dealing with the difficulties you encounter because of what you value. This may be the most difficult of the seven steps to implement. Acceptance is always the necessary first step toward resolving any conflict, but here it is the critical one, and, if you can manage it, the others will follow fairly easily. Accept that all others have the same rights to choose what they value as you do. All others. All values. The same rights as you. Even or especially when their systems totally contradict your own. This is very difficult to do, and few of us have been trained to be this accepting.

Accept that you can be wrong, for it is not human always to be right. If you yourself can be wrong, then so can some of your values. It is not important to be always right. It is not important always to win by convincing others that you are right and they are wrong, or misinformed. You can have wonderful values (truth, justice, fairness, love, peace, and so on), but if you act destructively while trying to communicate or force them upon others, you are denying them. Remember, you are less what you believe and value, and much more how you act and behave. If you can accept that no one else has to feel the same way as you about anything, you can begin to be accepting. If you can further allow others to think what they want, express their opinions as they choose, and believe they are right even when you know they are dead wrong, you can become an accepting listener. And if you can actually listen to your former opponent with open ears and a flexible mind, you can become wise and learned, a role model for others to follow. Acceptance is the critical key; without it you will remain stuck in years of futile arguments and wasted time and energy. Unless you are having fun and hurting no one, why bother to play the "I am right and you are wrong" game?

Recognize that your weak ego loves to get into arguments with those who believe differently than you do. It loves hasty negative impressions, quick judgments, and nasty criticisms. It thrives on finding differences with others and it needs to compare and judge. Your weak ego will grow as you become judgmental, critical, and negative. It will shrink when you become open, flexible, and understanding. Your weak ego is the mark of your insecurity; it accurately reflects the amount of self-esteem you lack. The more accepting you become, the less control your weak ego has over you. Recognize that accepting the rights of others to believe and value as they choose is not the same as condoning or capitulating to them. You can value what you choose, and accept that others will do the same. Acceptance is not agreement. It simply allows others to peaceably coexist with you. Accepting is simple, but never easy.

2. Letting Go

You do not have to let go of your value systems; instead let go of your attachment to them. In other words value what you want, as you recognize that this is your choice and not your need. Know that you are much more than what you believe and that you are choosing what you value, and that this is your decision at this moment in time. You do not have to convince others that what you have chosen is right or necessary for them. Let go of your attachment to conversion, and instead try to think of being a good role model. Let go of coercion or force, and allow others to emulate you or not, as they choose. Recognize that the more secure you are in your Self, the less you need to defend your values. And above all let go of judging others based on their different systems. All judgments and criticisms, unless solicited for constructive purposes by the person receiving the criticism, come from the weak ego, the insecure and unsure self.

As you become aware of the difference between having a facade and having a solid foundation, you will find it easier to let go of the problems associated with differences in others. The facade depends on the perceptions of others in order to function; your foundation is your own deep self and not dependent in any way upon anyone else. Others already see what you are;

let them see the reality of you rather than an image you are trying to project. Let go of the need to have others approve of what they see. Once you can do this, the facade will come tumbling down and the foundation will become more solid and sure. The great paradox here is that the more you can let go, the stronger you will become. The more accepting you become, the more others will choose to accept you and your values. Letting go will not take anything away from you; instead it will add to and enhance your life dramatically.

3. Expressing Feelings

Of the seven problem areas, this may well be the one in which expressing your feelings is the easiest step to do. Simply express all the feelings about your beliefs and values to yourself, by yourself, when you are alone or with someone who is supportive, nonthreatening, and not defensive about his own beliefs. Do not express your feelings to someone who violently opposes you or clearly lives and values things you feel are wrong. In other words express yourself when you will get no opposition; otherwise practice listening. You do not have to agree or condone or approve when you are listening; you only have to put your energy in your ears and not in your mouth or hands. If you can express your thoughts unemotionally, without intense feeling, you can discuss them with anyone. The more strongly you feel about what you are saying, the less you need to say it. Your emotions are yours, and you do not have to inflict them upon others unless you are very close or the other asks or expects you to do so. The exceptions to this are your family, lovers, and good friends; in these relationships intimacy depends upon being able to express your feelings. You do not have to be intimate with the community; you do not have to express everything you feel, especially that which is controversial.

4. Taking Responsibility

Taking responsibility for your values means that ultimately you own what you say, what you do, and the consequences of your actions. If you incite others to action, you are responsible for doing so. While it is true that you are not responsible for anything you cannot control, you must be aware that you can control what you believe and what you *do* with it. If you use it to manipulate others or cause secondhand destruction, you are responsible for creating a negative process. You are not absolved because you did not actually commit the behavior if your words created an action by another. If the other is a child, or vulnerable to you in any way, you are even more responsible for the consequences. If, however, the other has free choice and control and chooses to agree with your thinking, you are both equally responsible. For example if I instruct my child to go to school and steal some paper because I believe that stealing from institutions is not wrong, I am completely responsible for my child's behavior. I am also responsible for the training that I am giving this child. However, if I tell my spouse to steal paper from the office, both of us are responsible.

And if you are responsible, you can change because you have

control over yourself. You can retrain your values to match the way you feel about yourself. If you feel good, you will want your value system to correspond and reinforce your feeling. Begin slowly with things that are easy to change. Work up to the hard, critical values, the ones that cause the most difficulties for you. Question all of them. Take responsibility for the ones you keep. Change the ones that do not fit. You can do it!

You are responsible for your behavior when you create or foster negativity and discouragement in the community. While it is true that you cannot control how others feel or what they do, you can control whether you are encouraging or destructive. You do not live in a vacuum; what you say and do can have incredible effects upon others. Be true to yourself and you will not have to worry about the effect you have on others. In being true to yourself, you will have to recognize your innate goodness; once you can do this, it will become natural to perceive the goodness within others, even those who are diametrically opposed to your value systems. When you do confront evil, you will know it, and as appalled as you will be, you will not become vulnerable or susceptible to it. You will also not take responsibility for the choices of others, as you have learned that you cannot control them. You can only encourage them.

5. Forgiving

The need to forgive yourself for what you believe and value may at first seem abstract and unnecessary, unless you recognize that your actions develop from your thoughts and feelings. Because you can only forgive yourself for things that you first blame, meaning things that you are able to control and choose, and you cannot completely control your feelings and your thoughts, forgiveness in this instance would involve behavior and actions you have either committed or created. It is not always easy to distinguish what exactly is your part, that which is within your control, from what is not yours and not in your control. Suppose you believe that lying is wrong, but you lie to protect another: Have you committed an act that requires forgiveness?

These answers are never simple, as you will never know what is ultimately right or wrong in all cases. Perhaps the only way to resolve such thorny dilemmas is to try always to be true to your Self. In other words if you feel bad, you will need to forgive yourself. If you do not, because there is a larger justification that has caused you to act in opposition to your value system, you will not need to forgive yourself. An example of this might be if you did not believe in murder but you killed in order to protect your child. You may indeed feel justified in acting this way, even though it was against your beliefs. However, if you did feel that you were wrong, you will need absolution in order to move on.

The foregoing discussion raises the dilemma of not feeling responsible in those cases when you probably need to do so. This is easier to think about with regard to others than it is with yourself; you know of many cases where atrocities have been committed without conscience. But you can only deal with yourself, which is your lifetime's work. Because you do have a conscience, you must learn to trust it and do your best. Recognize that you will be wrong, you will do bad things, and you will hurt others. Forgive yourself for all of these and use your forgiveness as movement toward your change. Allow the discomfort that you feel when you do something that requires absolution to teach you not to do it again. Recognize that this is a lifelong process; life is composed of trial and error, practice, forgiveness, change, and growth.

Once you can forgive yourself, it is much easier to forgive others. There are some atrocities and evil that seem beyond the bounds of forgiveness. Sexual abuse of children, senseless killings, and genocide, to name a few, seem unforgivable. When you are confronted by incomprehensible violence, you may well need professional help to guide you and teach you objective eyes. You will never understand the reasons for much of the pain in this world. Perhaps understanding is not the task. The inability to forgive others creates a weight on your soul and stops you from living to the best of your abilities. When you are consumed with hatred, confusion, or the desire for revenge, you are no longer free, no longer involved with your own self-esteem, your own goodness. Something or someone else now has control of your soul. The ability to forgive nurtures your soul and frees your spirit. The inability to do so imprisons your soul and constricts your spirit. Which do you choose?

6. Appreciating

By now you may feel that the problems inherent in relating to the community are monumental and overwhelmingly negative. How can they possibly be appreciated? To begin with, you can appreciate the great diversity of beliefs in this world. At the very least they keep life interesting, and at the most they provide education and opportunities for enrichment. Think how bored you would be if everyone held similar beliefs and values. You can also be grateful that your choice of values allows you to belong in your society and communicate within your culture.

It might help to think of your belief and value systems as codes for communication, functioning in the same way as language. They work to unite you with those who understand the same codes, but they handicap you with those who do not. Just as language is not limiting when spoken in its culture, but quickly becomes so when taken to another, so also do value systems limit when they are out of context. An example of this is that in our Western culture status is earned or achieved, but in many other cultures status is ascribed or assigned. Learning and appreciating different systems can be much more difficult than learning a foreign language. You can appreciate that this interest and awareness is necessary, for both languages and values, if you want to communicate and relate. You are not limited when you expand your repertoire; in fact you are enhanced and made more versatile. You can certainly appreciate that!

Appreciate that there is much to learn outside your present awareness. And above all realize that you have the ability and the potential to learn. There are commonalities among all value systems; if you look for differences, you will easily find them, but they are usually only superficial. If you scratch the surface, you will find the similarities. Appreciate that these are what unite us and give us great joy. The appreciation of the beliefs and values of others will not limit or constrict you, but instead will enlarge and expand your vision and awareness. Isn't this another definition of growth and enhancement?

7. Rewarding

Now you arrive at the fun step. Reward yourself for being flexible. Reward yourself for your ability to allow others to believe and feel differently from you. Reward yourself for becoming wise. The recognition of what you are doing can be its own reward. You may find that your acceptance of others, your appreciation of them, your completion of the preceding steps have together produced many rewards that you could not have anticipated. Others may like you more, and they will certainly trust you more. You may already have found that you are a better listener and that you are learning much more now that you have become more open and flexible. You may feel rewarded that your new focus is on similarities rather than on differences. Certainly your feelings of belonging have increased because recognizing similarities creates feelings of togetherness while looking for differences creates separation and alienation. These are wonderful rewards indeed, and excellent reasons to begin.

You need continually to reward yourself in order for the entire process of self-esteem and social interest to keep occurring. Reward yourself by recognizing that what you have been doing as you worked through the preceding steps has been very difficult and against your previous training. It has certainly felt strange and at times uncomfortable. As you have persevered to any degree, you deserve a reward. Give it to yourself. Sometimes the simplest reward can be the most meaningful. By recognizing the difficulty of what you are doing, you are beginning the reward process. Pat yourself on the back. Smile at yourself in the mirror. Feel good about yourself. Why not? You deserve it. And, you will discover, it feels good. Say something nice to yourself; pay yourself compliments that you truly believe. It is amazing how easy it is to say "I am so stupid," but how difficult it is to say "I am great" or "I just did a wonderful thing."

Your training, combined with your weak ego, has taught you to look for differences, to criticize and judge both yourself and others, and to feel bad about many things. Whenever you go against your training and produce a positive change, you deserve a reward. The more internal rewards you can produce, the fewer external ones you will need. Your self-esteem requires encouragement (the giving of courage); rewarding yourself is one of the most encouraging activities you can engage in. As with all things, practice makes it easier. Practice throughout your day. Reward yourself every time you question your own values rather than judging those of others. Reward yourself very much each time you listen instead of debate. Especially reward yourself when you are able to remain calm in what would previously have been a heated confrontation. Above all reward yourself when your actions, beliefs, and values are all part of a cohesive and balanced, positive and esteemed, loving and loved you!

Your greatest reward will occur if you can practice the above. What you will discover by working your way through these steps is that you will finally belong. By being more accepting, you will be accepted, and while not always necessary, this acceptance always feels good. Being accepted is the icing on your cake. By letting go of your limitations, you will draw closer to others. When you take responsibility for what you control, you allow others to take their own responsibilities. By expressing your feelings appropriately, you will feel clean and safe, and others around you will also feel this way. Closeness will occur spontaneously. If you are able to forgive yourself for your limitations and imperfections, it will seem natural to forgive others for the same things. When you forgive them, they will be more likely able to forgive you. And when you demonstrate appreciation toward others, when you move past the differences and work toward finding the similarities, then you will discover the rewards of life and living, the joy of being, and the beauty inside all of us. If spirituality can be defined as the recognition of your own goodness and the appreciation of the goodness in others, then doing these things will make you a truly spiritual being. What could be more rewarding?

∽ Epilogue

This book begins with the premise that you will always have problems and that your life consists of dealing with your difficulties on a daily basis. Its intention is to change your focus from being overwhelmed by your problems to becoming an esteemed problem solver. In the process of doing so, you will have used seven steps, the same seven steps each time, to help you perceive your difficulties as challenges and to understand that they are part of your development—a necessary and affirming aspect of your growth. These steps function at three different levels, each of which has its own purpose, somewhat independent of the others. The first, most basic level, is to utilize the problem-solving steps as just that—to help resolve or cope with your difficulties. They will certainly work to give you a sense of mastery, to identify what you can and cannot control, and to help you deal with your ever-occurring problems. The steps are specific enough to allow you to recognize where you are in your resolution process and exactly what you need to work on. They are general enough to cover all possibilities and allow you to recognize your involvement in the process of living. If you only use them at this level, you will benefit, as you will learn to perceive your problems as developmental necessities and to know that you can cope.

However, these steps also function at another level, perhaps a higher, more abstract one. They work to teach you how to *be*. They clearly show you how to move beyond your cultural training that you must always be doing in order to be successful, and they help you discover the balance and peace inherent in being. This is especially true of the first two steps—accepting and letting go—because Being is all about acceptance and detachment. When you learn to do this with your problem, you are also learning to do this with yourself. You can generalize the process from the one specific area that you are working on to the whole of your life. You will do this even if you are not exactly aware of what you are doing. When you know your own mind and are able to express your feelings to yourself, you become real. If you can accept the reality of one small part of your life, you have opened the door to acceptance of all of it. If you can learn to let go of your illusions, expectations, and guilt in the one instance, you will have learned how to do so again, until you can do so in all situations. Just as each of your problems presents an opportunity to be challenged and to learn, so also does each of your problem-solving skills. When you are working on your difficulties, you are simultaneously working on your life. If you asked for specific action steps to teach you how to *Be*, these seven problem-solving steps would be the ones. How wonderful that you get double advantage: You use the steps to solve your problems and you learn how to *Be* at the same time!

But this is not all. There is a third level on which you can use these seven steps—perhaps the most rewarding one. This level deals with developing spirituality, living your goodness, and recognizing your connection to God. These seven steps are highly related to the process of developing self-esteem. You learn to love yourself by accepting the reality of your Self, your goodness, and by letting go of the need for perfection. You learn to live your goodness when you take responsibility, make amends, and forgive yourself. You learn to reinforce the process and practice of being esteemed when you appreciate and reward yourself. You become actively involved in the development of encouragement; you are accepting your imperfections and at the same time recognizing your worth. When you do this with others, which is exactly what these steps allow you to learn and practice in your relationships, you develop social interest. When you recognize your own goodness (self-esteem) and acknowledge the goodness within others (social interest), you become a spiritual being. You begin by trying to solve problems and end by becoming spiritual. God works in wonderful ways!

These seven steps are not limited to problem-solving relationships. They will work for all problems. My book *The Portable Problem Solver: Coping with Life's Stressors* discusses the use of these steps in dealing with the other stressful issues of life. In it I cover the problems of work, money, time, change, prejudice, disease, and death. The seven problem-solving steps are the same as the ones in this book. However, the ways in which they can be applied will change, depending upon the circumstances. The more you practice your problem-solving skills, the better you will be able to deal with this crazy and often confusing world. But above and beyond coping, when you use these steps, you practice the process of self-esteem, you encourage the development of social interest, you are actively Being and are making the most of Doing—you become spiritual. Seven steps that do so much. How can you not want to use them?

A final way to think of these steps is as seven guides toward actively loving. They help to solve your problems by teaching the power of love, the practice of love, and the process of love. They teach you to understand your connections—to your Self, with others, and toward God. These steps will take you out of the passive, waiting for something to happen, and move you into action, particularly internal activity. They serve as a continual reminder that life is process, you are always changing, and that your journey is in this moment. Moreover they reinforce you for doing what you can and being aware of what you are. If you are using them, you are doing your best, you are living your goodness, you are Being. That is all you can ever do, and it is enough!